Exploring the Art of Puppet Theater

Paul Vincent Davis

With drawings by

John Lechner

cp

Text copyright © 2018 by Paul Vincent Davis.
Drawings copyright © 2018 by John Lechner.

All rights reserved. No part of this book may be reproduced in any form or by any electronic or mechanical means, including information storage and retrieval systems, without permission in writing from the publisher, except by reviewers who may quote brief passages in a review.

ISBN: 978-0-921845-48-5

Library and Archives Canada Cataloguing in Publication Data

Davis, Paul Vincent, author

    Exploring the art of puppet theater / Paul Vincent Davis ; with drawings by John Lechner.

ISBN 978-0-921845-48-5 (softcover)

1. Puppet theater. 2. Puppets. 3. Puppet making. I. Title.
II. Title: Exploring the art of puppet theater.

PN1972.D38 2018   791.5'3   C2018-904400-4

Charlemagne Press
Garden Bay, BC
V0N 1S1 Canada

Dedicated with great love and respect for

Mary Phipps Putnam Churchill

1930 - 1996

Founder of the Puppet Showplace Theater

June 4, 1974.

What is inside the chest?

Table of Contents

	Prelude	VII
1	Reality and Fantasy	1
2	Lies That Tell the Truth	9
3	Hands Up! This is a Puppet Play	19
4	Superstar Understudy	31
5	Fingers Do the Talking	37
6	A Twist of the Wrist	47
7	Puppets Up in Arms	55
8	Nobody Becomes a Who	67
9	Curtain Raisers • Episodes • Mini-Dramas	75
10	Props & Props Alive	83
11	The Breath of Life	95
12	Speaking in Voices	101
13	Acting Up	111
14	Which Comes First?	121
15	Building Blocks of Theater	131
16	Mini-Dramas • Playlets • Etudes	135
17	Etudes in B#	143
18	Write It All Out	149
19	Be a Pro	157
	Postlude	168

Paul Vincent Davis with a character from
The Leprechan of Donegal.

Prelude

A life-long love of the visual arts, theater, music, and dance led me into the arts and skills of puppetry, which is a wonderful melding of all the arts. Within that creative blending, puppet theater is its own separate and fulfilling art form.

In creating and performing with puppet figures for twenty-five years as a child, teen and young adult amateur, and fifty years as a professional puppet artist, I have learned and used many classical and traditional formats, discovered new and more modern techniques and created a few techniques of my own to accomplish fine theater, and to offer the art of puppetry as a creative theater art.

Puppetry is both a visual and a literary art of communication through playwriting, sculpture, painting, costuming, scenic design, vocal and choreographic arts. The results are dramatic, humorous, rich artistic performances. Puppet theater is, and must be, a vital and meaningful communication between the audience and the creators of the work, whether a solo piece or fully staffed group. That communication is the vitality of puppet theater.

This book reaches beyond today's often limited vision of this amazing art form. Puppet theater is not an imitation of human theater nor a simplistic variation of it. Puppet theater is its own rich and vibrant theatrical form. This book reaches past the simple mechanics of puppetry to explore how the artist's mind grasps and shapes every element of the puppet play. It is my dream actors, puppeteers, directors, singers, dancers, visual artists, sculptors and orchestra conductors will explore and rediscover the full potential of puppetry as an amazing visual and dramatic theater art.

First, I will examine the ideology and some concepts of the history of fine visual arts, so puppetry can take its place in this realm.

Together we will explore crafting characters, visually, then give the character voice and trace the genesis of a puppet play, from idea, writing, rehearsing and into the final form. Then I will explore the professional practices that polish the artistic endeavor into the finished work.

This book also expresses my long lived dream and hope that fine theaters – on, off, and far afield from Broadway, across the nation and around the world – will offer experimental, artistic and creative works of puppet theater in their programming.

There have been many eras in the past when puppet theater was more widely performed, but in today's modern theater, it is not happening. There has been much fine puppetry in theaters and art centers of Europe, Russia, Canada and South America, but only a relative few in the United States offer commanding puppet theater works for adult audiences.

Some very fine American groups are working toward this goal, but not enough. These dreams are shared with the hope of reaching out to audiences around the world. A few professional theaters include puppetry in their presentations, but they are extremely rare.

Most puppetry in the United States is created as individual and personal ideology. Many of the performers create puppetry as solo or two puppeteer performances, which may be magnificent when well done, but as a primary viewpoint, it is limiting to puppet theater as a fully developed and vital art form.

A few colleges and universities offer degrees in puppet theater in their Art and Theater Departments, and they are accomplishing wonderful and challenging approaches to puppet theater. A few opera productions have used puppets in scenes of transition during long instrumental sections, but even those are infrequent.

As I pursue these goals, I will be relying on glove puppets, my specialty, to illustrate my points. Glove puppets are the most difficult of all puppet styles to perform with artistic merit. I have also chosen to focus on the glove puppet since it cannot be truly realistic in its form or function. The figures cannot look or move as humans do and the illusions created must be constantly reinvented, reviewed anew and rediscovered, stylized, imagined and designed to make audiences believe in the artful reality of the puppet object. These elements make them an ideal case study to better understand the depth of artistry involved in puppet theater. If you specialize in another form of puppetry, the concepts and artistic thought processes I will discuss may be adapted to the creative practices of puppet creators' art form. What is vital is to consider the how and why behind every element of puppet theater, no matter the type of puppet used.

While a glove puppet and other puppet style, may only look and move like a puppet, it may still strongly and vitally reach out to stir the audience's emotions, feelings and philosophies. My aim is to equip puppeteers to develop their skills in the worthy and vigorous art form of puppet theater.

The great playwright Moss Hart wrote about Broadway theater, and his thoughts encompass the attitude needed to excel in the fine art of puppetry: "The only credential the city of New York asked was the boldness to dream. For those who did, it unlocked its gates and its treasures, not caring who they were or where they came from."

Paul Vincent Davis
Artist in Residence Emeritus,
Puppet Showplace Theater
Brookline, MA

Samurai from
Folk Tales of Japan.

1   Reality and Fantasy

Pablo Picasso, the renowned Spanish artist, noted: "Anything the human mind can imagine is real." The truth of Picasso's statement may be found in the gazillions of bizarre images created by the active and vital human imagination from the cave dwellers at the beginnings of humankind to the present day and all the times in between that we know, guess, dream or hope to be true.

This truism is just as viable to puppet theater as it is to any art form. Thus, we begin here, in an exploration of what art is, in its basic form, and what it aspires to do. Without this perspective, a puppeteer may not give or gain the most out of the art of puppet theater.

The statement is evident in humanity's long history of constantly searching for details from all unrecorded times, wiser times, brilliant times, the wild and less learned times, the times of rediscovery and the search for answers to new and ancient vital questions, wonders, discoveries, hopes, dreams and wisdom of the many later centuries and human cultures.

People change with the times and the times with the people. We are all taken by new events, discoveries and movements into the future, and we are equally mystified by the people, ways and means of times long past. Art reflects its own time and inspires the arts of the future.

All of this has brought us into the technologies and sciences of today. The study of man's accomplishments throughout history brings forth a wide scope of foolishness and error in the search for answers to the never ending list of questions, wonders, unbelievable truths, lauded lies, denied realities, needs, joys and adversities of life, love, arts and politics surrounding us from ancient times to the present day. Ancient images, distortions and variations of the living creatures in the natural world, including feral and domesticated beings, insects, birds, sea creatures, beasts plus a myriad of imagined creations all carved or painted in caves, on rocks and high cliff walls, may be imaginative, boring, magical, natural, good or evil, mortal or immortal, moral or immoral, comical or tragic. All brilliant distortions of images and representations of vital interest, as humanity asks questions and seeks answers to life's multiple and often unanswered and unanswerable questions.

With all the variations of time, much stays the same. We humans still paint our names, code names and pictures on buildings with cliff-like walls. We carve our lover's names on trees, and love to hear our echoes bouncing from cliff to rocky peak.

Cultures too, echo the common threads of human existence. The sphinx, basilisk, griffon, hydra, centaur, minotaur, Cyclops, the Yeti (Abominable Snowman) and its cousin the Sasquatch (Big Foot), mermaids, mermen, and myriads of variations of super to substandard humans in the forms of giants, ogres, sorcerers, witches, fairies, trolls, gnomes, Will o' the Wisps, vampires, goblins and goons, all appear in folk lore, mythology, fairy tales, fine literature, learned and modern imaginative fabrications, fine and folk arts, films and novels from around the world and in every known cultural community.

We have both humorous and scary clowns, Santa Claus, the Boogeyman, the Easter Bunny, Tooth Fairy, that monster in the closet or under the bed, and other imaginative creatures to tantalize us, create wonder, wisdom, laughs and lies for ourselves and our children to imagine, love, hate, fear and question.

Ghosts, spirits, ghouls, hobgoblins, bugbears, witches flying on broomsticks, and outer space aliens flying in giant saucers are all said to venture about on dark and spooky nights, in dreams and nightmares that may come to terrorize us by the light of the moon when telling tales of terror, toasting marshmallows and eating s'mores around the blazing campfire.

We have broken turkey bones, a wish at the first slice of a birthday cake, good luck charms, wishing rings, four leaf clovers, and wishing wells of coins in the carved marble fountains of times gone by and the many small pools of water in public places. We have magic spells, hope chests, dream catchers, lucky charms, magic hats and lucky souvenirs to make our hopes and dreams come true. Not to neglect Superman, Super Woman, Captain Marvel, The Hulk and at least a hundred more super heroes of wise and worthy comic book artists and publishers.

Dragons appear in the images and stories of many cultures around the world. They are said to fly on great bat like-wings and breathe fire when angry. No living creature is capable of breathing fire, yet fire itself is, and has always been, a life and property threatening terror while simultaneously offering the comforts of warmth, physical, mental and emotional pleasure. In Asia dragons are the living images of thunder, lightning and rain and the great silver dragon of tidal waters splashing vibrantly upon the shores. Again, all are highly destructive and frightening, while at the same time supplying water for the trees, plants, farms, animals, humans, and grand cities of today's modern lands and the oceans that surround us.

It seems art, and the many imaginations it springs from, is as varied as it is uniform. From these roots, puppet artists, along with all humans, draw their dreams and imaginations grow. Albert Einstein

once quipped, "Logic will take you from point A to point B. Imagination will take you anywhere."

He advised parents to encourage their children to read folklore and fairy tales where knowledge, discovery, imagination and reality all embrace and comprehend one another. These fairy tales and folkloric pieces also defy, condemn, distract from and encourage the mind to stretch into many other depths of the thinking process, the mind, the heart and spirit of the reader.

Neither reality nor fantasy is ever simply what it is. Imagination discovers and rediscovers both fantasy and reality through facts, fancies, hopes, dreams, fears, lies and truths. Reality is hidden within the many truths and within secrets waiting for discovery, hiding somewhere within the realm of fantasy. Yesterday and today humankind has questioned both reality and fantasy while both continue to shape our outlooks on the meaning and reason for life.

Imagination is not far removed from reality, but is, and must be, a vital way of looking at truth through a magnifying lens, discovering the wonderful variants within a complex whole while looking for the truth within the cracks, chips and leaks of the splintered shape of reality.

Einstein also reminds us to, "Never stop questioning." That is the heart of any endeavor, and it is the approach we will take to puppet theater in this book.

Imagination is simply another way of discovering and rediscovering the worlds of fantasy and reality, lies and truths that have hounded us throughout our human existence.

We as humans each have our own personal appearance. Our eyes, ears, noses, mouths hands, feet, hair and skin colors are all different and very personal. None of us looks exactly like another, a prominent doctor recently announced no two human ears are exactly alike. I suspect that is true of all human parts, no two are ever the same.

Even identical twins are not the same: one is the first born, the other later by minutes or hours, and while there may be strong similarities in appearance there are also many minute variations. One twin is often nicer, and one may have a stronger or weaker personality, one may be more foolish or wiser, or are parted from being identical by many other minor differences.

Since yesterday, a thousand years ago and tomorrow, anyone's hair may be any color or mélange of colors desired by drying wet hair in the heat of the sun, the use of mud, bleach, bull urine (a common practice in Medieval times), dyes, permanent and temporary colorings, by braiding, implanting hair of real or artificial construction.

Hair may be straightened, curled, fluffed, puffed and twisted, braided, cut, shaved away entirely, artfully designed or carelessly wild, covered with powdered or varicolored wigs, draped to be completely hidden from sight, combed out neatly or left to be crazy wild by design, desire and, of course, by fashion. All of that is only in the hair.

With all of our many differences and variations, we humans are still all very much alike. We are all kindred. We are all brothers and sisters of the same human race. With our thousands of similarities and differences, we are all still human beings, all akin.

Why and how we love and hate one another is a question of the comprehensions of our surrounding society and its varied ideals, intents and attempts at survival and the powerful forces within our brilliant insanities and insensitive dreams, and many of our fulfilled and unrealized hopes.

Everyone outside of our own cave clan is foreign and to be feared, hated, avoided and even killed. Other outsiders may be loved and romanced with joy, delight and fervor because they are different and thus, somehow, better. They become other, outré and very interesting!

We humans, are extremely variable, changeable and flexible. Wisdom is part of our way of moving on despite the complexities of living and the fragility and brevity of life itself. Art both reflects and challenges these realities, and puppet theater is no different.

Picasso's statement at the beginning of this chapter is both fantasy within reality and reality beyond the make-believe of fairy tales which, though make-believe, often have many hidden realities and truths hidden within them.

A favorite old joke offers this piece of human wisdom, reflecting the contradictions of human existence and thought: "It has been said that we are all descended from the apes. Let us hope it is not true! However, if it is true, we must hope and pray the neighbors don't find out."

"What fools these mortals be," said Puck from *A Midsummer Night's Dream* by Shakespeare. Thus, from this place of foolishness that is utterly human, we forget art – from paintings to puppets –

which are expressive, enhancing and challenging to our very nature.

Caterpillar from
A Musical Variety.

2 Lies That Tell the Truth

Pablo Picasso and Constantin Stanislavsky have each expressed the view: "All art is a lie that tells the truth." Art has been a vital part of human society since the earliest days of human existence from the end of the Ice Age and gamboling through eons of time, changing thought, images, formats and techniques at every turn. To truly develop the depth of the art form of puppetry, each puppeteer – and the field as a whole – must take its place in this vital procession of human creativity.

Art rendered on cave walls and carved on the sides of mountain cliffs was a form of conversation, explanation, and vital communication. With no strongly developed language or techniques for writing, those early primitive peoples created paintings, drawings and carvings to convey information often using lifeless stick figures for the humans while the animals were pictured with far more grace and communicative details. Why? No one knows.

Possibly because the human viewer would know human appearance but the animals were the informative parts of the pictures and therefore more carefully and sensitively pictured. The artwork might also have been created to communicate with the spirits of the slaughtered beasts to thank them for allowing the people to kill them for food, clothing and protection.

We humans still paint our names, code names, signatures and good and bad murals on walls of cliff-like buildings, fences, doors and barns and gigantic billboards blocking our view of the beautiful and startling countryside beyond.

Art's primary function is, as it has always been, a form of communication. Puppet theater is no different. Art is often a duplication of the reality or image of life, as in some fine portraiture. Art may also be a reevaluation of a visual, mental and/or emotional reality, inspired within the personal visions and interpretations of the many art techniques of pictorial imagery.

When looking at a great painting by a master artist, one is not, necessarily, seeing what the artist saw, but rather the artist's interpretation or vision of what is before her or him. The artist expresses the art from within the self, using the many techniques from training, practice and life's own influences. Art, like human behavior, changes with the times wherein it is created.

The viewers' inner responses to the art recreates it and makes it new, fresh and vital, or hated, despised and reevaluated with every viewing. We each see art through our own eyes. Our individual minds discover, rediscover and deny or praise art as we see it.

Art is the rendered picture of emotional and personal vision and often a suggestion of reality, artistic interpretation and, all too often, an overeager grabbing at a currantly popular art style and the rejection of styles from times gone by. Of course, there is also inspiration issuing from any new form.

Art may be magnificently beautiful or hideously ugly depending on the many ideas of those trying to explain it. Art is influenced by the art training studios, expressions of art impresarios or critical personal opinions, whether true, false or misunderstood. It is influenced by the techniques of art styles and the blended colors and color relationships, light and dark tones and textures of the paint, the quality of the brush strokes hinting at the light of the sun, the candle, modern electric lighting, the dark of night, or the rich beauty of the light of the moon and a million other pictured images and painterly techniques. Puppetry, too, has these intricacies of communication, and beauty. Art is a powerful form of communication, a philosophy and a visual realization which may be created in countless ways. All the expressions of life, history and haunting new views into an unknown future, and sometimes secrets, moods and inner feelings.

Many paintings and sculptures of seeming photographic realism reveal secrets in almost invisible ways. Strokes of the brush, tints, tones and textures of the paints. The strikes of the hammer on the chisel chipping wood, marble, stone or metal and the clay molded by pressures of the fingers of the hand. The artist's mental and emotional impressions, attitudes of the times expressed, distorted or beautifully revealed in the image of a work of art. Artists wield these layers of meaning to cause the audience to question, to explore.

For example, in a painting of the early eighteenth century, a child is shown dressed in a full and formal hoop skirted gown with yards of silk and lace, with a white powdered wig tied up with ribbons, all the high fashions of the day. The child is beautifully realized in the center of the canvas. Just outside of the room through a door, in vague images, almost in shadow, are the parents and servants at attention, tense, concerned, waiting in case they are called upon for some unknown need. The artist himself is dimly reflected in a mirror in the back of the room, almost (but not quite) hidden behind his easel and the backside of the canvas on which he is in the process of painting the child's image.

On looking at the painting, one must to ask, "Why?" The artist might have simply painted the fashionably overdressed child in the empty room, as a portrait, but he did not, would not, or could not stop at the usual, and went on into the deeper truths, asking multiple visual and mental questions but giving no answers.

In the Italian Renaissance the artists discovered the Camera Obscura. A panel with a small hole that refracts the light and projects a living image onto the surface of a stretched and primed canvas. The artist then traces the image as it is reflected and paints the image within their own art style and technique. Is the artist cheating or is he discovering a new and experimental technique? A bit of both in all probabilities.

A Dutch painting depicts a routine and simple domestic scene, but there is a shadowy image of someone in a large hat, outside, looking in through the shadowed window of a door. The figure is almost unnoticeable unless the viewer looks very closely. Who is this shadowy person obviously spying on the simple scene, and why? The answer is not given.

El Greco's painting of a great and powerful Cardinal shows the prelate posing in his crimson gown and cap, a golden chain and the medallion of his station on his breast. He is sitting in an elaborately carved throne-like chair. The Cardinal is regal in his surroundings expressing calm control, yet his right hand is gripping the handle of the chair so tightly that his knuckles have turned white. Why? The artist has asked, the viewers must seek the answer for themselves.

These intentional, mysterious questions are central to the communication between artists and audience. Puppet theater must bring its own questions and invite its audience to delve into the mysteries of artificial puppet theater projecting realistic aspects of life and its many wonders.

Abstract paintings also have mood, mental, physical, emotional and visual intents. We often see beyond reality in a visual perception of non-pictorial tensions and the shaping and expression of the artist's hidden fears, hopes, dreams or nightmares which may create both positive and/or negative effects on the viewer causing unexpected emotions from within the viewer's inner self.

Again, it is the brush strokes, the texture of the paint, the colors, the non-pictorial visual images that touch and move the emotions of the viewer in multiple, intellectual, emotional and, sometimes, amazingly confusing reactions.

Van Gogh's painting of sunflowers is a greatly beloved painting. It is the rich texture of the thick paint in the broad brush strokes which makes the image vibrate off the canvas and land in the minds and hearts of the viewers. The seeming insanity of the artist and the visual joy of the painting are one.

One abstract painting is simply a canvas painted flat white with a single broad stroke of black paint smeared on with a very broad bristled brush. On studying the painting at a distance, the eye perceives a battle between the white canvas and the black splash of paint, as if each is striving, indeed fighting, for dominance as the primal and focal visual image.

In many centuries of painting, white is a strong focal and foreground color while black is a recessive shadowy color. By transposing the black smear onto a white background, the eye is tricked and fooled, the art process is twisted, and competes with the eye of the viewer.

So it is in all forms of art. Every work of art is unique within itself. A book is often unlike the film based on the story and actions within the book. Ballet differs from any other forms of dancing, a fine poem is quite dissimilar from a rich song lyric, puppets are often used to recreate a classic play originally for live actors, the artificiality of the puppet objects changes the effect of the play upon the audience. A comic opera is quite dissimilar from a musical comedy, a piano sonata has little relationship to a jazz riff, a folk tune or a rock inspired piano piece.

A play for children is not the same as a play intended for adults. Every art form exists within its own specific demands and qualities.

Some overlapping of techniques and skills are vital, but no two art forms are ever quite alike. Every art is simply itself whether complex or simple, it has its own controls, its own mental and visual images and its own powers of communication and effects on the viewers' emotions.

As puppeteers delve deeply into their art form, they cannot shy away from these complexities and layers of meaning. They must intentionally and thoughtfully adapt their methods and meanings to the abilities and inabilities of the art form to create something wholly unique for the audiences to discover.

One puppet play is unlike another, even of the same title, tale and characters because the artist is recreating the tale and wants the art to be their own, or maybe sees the intent of the tale in a new or personal way to be shared with the audience.

There are many obvious and subtle changes in creating a performance for the self, and creating a performance for a group of puppeteers. A puppet play is still more varied with the type of puppet figure used, and different yet again with the individual creator's intent for the play, and variable again through the performer's viewpoint and audience's current interests and needs.

The same is true of a theater group adapting any play from Shakespeare. The director makes it his own, the designer creates new visual continuity for the figures, costuming, scenic design and all visual aspects of the play. The actors recreate the characterizations in new ways to make the play their own.

The vitality of good puppet theater lies in the tools of the art form. A marionette and a glove puppet cannot physically move or act in the same way! A glove puppet may open a door, pass through it and shut the door behind itself. A marionette has strings that cannot pass through a door frame. The stringed figure, however, can walk, fly or spin eloquently in a dance routine and sit easily in a

hand carved chair, while the glove must fake a walk without legs, and certainly cannot spin nor fly, because there is a living puppeteer's arm inside the figure to move it, but prevents flight, acrobatics or balletic *pirouettes or* the simple act of *sitting* on a chair.

Seeing a play performed by sculpted and painted figures is no less an art than live actors on stage, but they *are* not, *may* not, *should* not, and *cannot* be the same. A glove puppet is its own existence, with no capabilities beyond its own visuality. The puppeteer with the glove figure, may create a million truths within the lies of performance, but not the same lies and truths of the marionette, a rod puppet or a shadow figure and in no way like a human being.

Puppetry must come from the heart and soul of the puppet artist using the figures, just as the painted art on canvas or paper, or sculptures carved of wood, marble, metal or stone, must be the artist's touch to stir the souls, minds and hearts of the viewers.

So must the constructed image of the puppet and its artificial realities inspired by giving and retelling of the human images, touching the hearts and spirits of the audience members.

The one thing a glove puppet rarely accomplishes well is the attempt to be realistic. It has been tried, is often attempted, but realism in glove puppet theater rarely works, because glove puppetry is within itself an artificially created image incapable of duplicating the dynamic moves of humanity. The glove figure may suggest them, reinterpret them, reinvent or create new techniques to suggest reality, but the glove puppet figure is fantasy in form and function.

There is a wonderful Yiddish folk tale where the people proclaimed how they loved truth and questioned fantasy. So Truth went to visit the ones who said they loved Truth. The people, seeing the ugly, naked truth, were horrified, frightened and embarrassed and came to distrust and fear the truth. Many of them turned to the more beautiful trivialities of Fantasy.

At some point the lonely and ugly Truth meets the newly beloved and beautiful Fantasy. Truth and Fantasy fell in love and from then until now both Truth and Fantasy are loved as one together, but never as one alone.

All tales must have some of the strong reality of Truth and some of the invented lies and joys of Fantasy.

Glove puppetry may still be turned into a wonderfully believable fantasy but it always needs the reality of truth within it to make it viable. It is in the portrayal of the storied content by using the puppet object that makes the *play* a rich art form for all ages, from the nursery to the costly theaters on, off and far afield from Broadway.

That the puppets are constructed images is known, recognized and hopefully enjoyed as artful sculpture. The skill of the puppet performer using the voice, fingers, wrists and arms to convey a good story is the joy of glove puppet theater. It is also the shared or offset togetherness of Fantasy and Truth that wins the heart. *All art is a lie that tells the truth.*

The Ugly Truth & Beautiful Fantasy

To achieve the best of fine puppet theater, the artist must consider all these ideas before delving into the practicalities of producing a show. The puppet is an instrument for communicating and sharing with an audience, controlled and moved by a human puppeteer. The puppets are not the performers of fine puppet theater, the puppeteers acting the words, rendering the story through the movements and suggested emotions of the puppet figures, are the true performers of the puppet play using puppets as the *illustrations* for the tales being shared with the audiences through vocal and emotional acting and manipulation. This giving and sharing is the artistry of imagination from within to enjoy, celebrate, share and refocus on the artistry of fine puppet theater.

Little Red Riding Hood

3 Hands Up! This is a Puppet Play!

All forms of puppet theater communicate with the audience through the gift of rich, visual, imaginative and meaningful performance. The audience responds to the gift of that story and its characters with laughter, gasps, tears and other responses throughout the play and again at the curtain call, sometimes even with thrilling standing ovations.

Puppet theater is no simple act. To master the art form requires deep thought, careful practice and enriched, visually compelling storytelling. This section will cover some of the basic mechanics of puppetry and the crafting of a puppet character, beginning with simple movement in this chapter, but do not forget that even the most elementary skills must be accomplished with great attention to the artistic aims of the performance.

The Puppet as Object

The puppet is *not* an object pretending to be a human. A puppet is a creative and artistic *illustration* of a specific character within a story, play or performance. Good theater is never a pretense, a trivial or meaningless diversion. It is a recreation of an idea about life, whether real, distorted or fantastic. It is a powerful form of communication between the author, director and performers and, of course, the audience.

The performer's hands, arms and body must skillfully move the puppets through their choreographed performances with controlled intent, artistry, dexterity and something akin to passion, with a strong sense of communication and sharing. The performer must be in good physical, mental and emotional control to accomplish these goals! A little creative insanity is also part of rich and vital puppet theater. The puppet is not the performer of the play. It is the puppeteer's illustration of his or her puppet presentation. The puppeteer is the performer of any and all puppet presentations.

Tricks of the Trade

The puppeteer must move and manipulate *without* pain or harm to the self. This requires frequent exercises for fluidity and the believability of each movement of the puppet as well as sensitivity to characteristic and personalities within the tale. All this must be accomplished by a skilled and well trained performer with the intent to share and inspire the viewers.

While every move of the puppet is choreographed to inform the audience, the puppeteer performer is free to change, enhance or perfect a choreographed move for clearer and richer communication even while contending with the form and limitations of the puppet.

Human vs. Puppet Movement

Somebody's Fingers, Hands & Arms

The following exercises may help to develop the puppeteer's physical performance needs. Doing these exercises backstage before a rehearsal and/or performance is a good way to keep the blood flowing in the hands and to relax the hands, arms and back. The exercises will aid in performing with artistry and safe, secure moves. The exercises are important for learning to move, control and express through the arms, hands and fingers without excessive pain caused by tension in new or difficult movements. These exercises are specifically designed for glove puppeteers, but they and other similar exercises may be adapted, and are vital, for all forms of puppetry.

Get the Blood Flowing and the Hands Relaxed

Stand tall and straight, relaxed and without tension. Shake the hands in the air from the wrists for approximately five to ten-seconds. This is useful whenever the hands feel tense or stiff. This exercise is usable any time (out of audience view). Do not overdo this exercise as the hands or wrists could eventually become sore or tired.

Hold the hand flat like an artist's palette, palms down, fingers together while keeping the elbows relaxed and slightly down. Now slowly spread the fingers as wide and far apart as possible. Hold the hands still and feel the tension in the hands and fingers in the stretch. Without moving the hands or changing the hand position, consciously and mentally feel the tension in the hands and fingers slowly fade away until the hands, still widely spread, are relaxed and comfortable. Slowly close the hands into tightly clinched but relaxed and tension free fists. Repeat this several times until it is easy to stretch the fingers and clinch the fist without tension.

Perform this exercise (at least once a day) to keep full control of stretching without strain. This elimination of tension is needed for all puppet types.

In many situations the puppet figure must often express various physical and emotional tensions, which the performer must learn to create and present to the audience without feeling personal tensions.

Exercises for Flexibility and Fluidity

Hold both hands palms down, flat like an artist's palette, fingers together, elbows slightly bent, relaxed. Starting with the writing hand, point the thumb down to the floor, hold it for a moment or two, then bring it back to the original position. Now the pointer finger by itself, pointing straight down to the floor below. Hold it for a moment then return to the flat hand position. Remember to keep the fingers relaxed and consciously avoid tension.

Continue on with each finger one at a time pointing down to the floor and then relaxing. Now do the same with the non-writing hand, one finger at a time. Practice both hands together, one finger after the other.

Experiment, play with this one, make a game of it. Point the thumb of one hand and the little finger of the other and continue with all the fingers. The important part is to do these moves without tension. Tension will occur at times in any performing situation, the idea is to use that tension dramatically and then allow it to soften.

Expressive Moves

The following exercise is good for strong control and drilling the hands in moving only one finger at a time, while also eliminating unnecessary tension and developing the flexibility for communication through the puppet figure. Holding the hands flat, fingers wide apart but without tension, move each finger one after the other in a full circle five times. Make an effort to keep the hand and the other fingers very still. Each finger, one after the other, makes a full circular movement five times. This is usually difficult the first few times, but with effort and practice it will run smoothly. This exercise is also usable to help control the hands in moving only one finger at a time and to strengthen the fingers to keep the hands flexible and fluid in performance.

The Stroke and the Scoop

Both the Stroke and the Scoop movements are from Corporeal Mime. These exercises are to strive for discipline and control without tension and they are very useable moves within the glove puppet for some actions. Each step of the movement must be done fully, completely and smoothly. Done slowly these moves are very elegant and fluid, performed rapidly they may suggest a sense of urgency and may be adapted into the choreography.

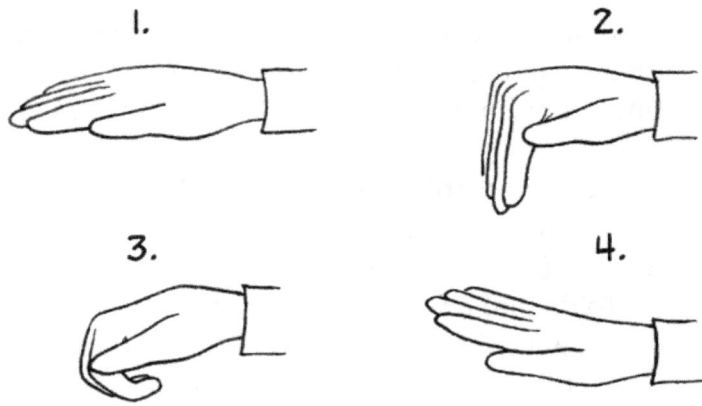

The Stroke: The Stroke move is very much like stroking the fur of a pet with controlled moves.

1. Hold the arm and hand palm down, fingers together, flat like an artist's palette.
2. Fold the fingers down from the major knuckles to form a vertical wall. Keep the wrist still and straight.

3. Fold the fingers into a fist (without tension)
4. Now uncurl the fingers to form a very wide "V" shape at the wrist. Elbow up.
5. Level the hand and arm back to form the original flat palette.

Practice each of these parts to flow gracefully one from the other.

Do not allow the moves to become sloppy.

The steps are very specific and must be done cleanly and fluidly as described.

The Scoop: The Scoop movement is similar to the Stroke move in reverse.

The move is like scooping the hand through finely ground corn meal or in the sand of a sandbox with the palms down. It is almost, but not quite the reverse of the Scoop move.

1. Like the Stroke, the hand is held palms down, perfectly flat as the artist's palette.
2. The fingers move down to form the wall, and the hand then folds into a fist and the wrist moves up as the elbow goes down.
3. Now the hand uncurls, makes a scooping move as if digging in soft sand the wrist bends down and the elbow moves up forming a strong "V".
4. Now the back of the hand, the wrist and the elbow bend level one with the other into the flat palette.

Practice the *Stroke* and the *Scoop* movements in different ways, always being certain to do each part of the move cleanly, correctly and with complete control. Try for smooth, flexible and very relaxed hands during the move. Perform the *Stroke* moves to the side like *Lovely Hula Hands*. Work exaggerated *Scoop* moves like fish diving in and out of the water and then have the fish swimming across the stage. The important thing is to do each part of these moves cleanly, specifically and gracefully. Do not get sloppy or careless. The accuracy and fluidity of these moves is the *heart and soul* of the intent.

The Tool of the *Tuk*

Tuk is a term and move also borrowed from Corporeal Mime. The word was originally "tuh" with a hard accent on the uh and over time it evolved into "tuk." The tuk is, simplistically, a visual punctuation-like addition within a move which shapes, clarifies or intensifies an important emotional gesture, reaction or change of mood or meaning.

The tuk has many variations and is frequently a minute physical move or a pause with an edge to it. It might be at the beginning, within or at the end of a complex move. The tuk may be soft, medium or hard depending on the force or strength of the move and/or intent of the visual communication.

The tuk is essential at times in puppet movement in order for the audience to see, comprehend and emotionally respond within a complicated or multifaceted move. This move gives importance to a puppet action. It is also a visual stress, a visual tag of emotional expression. Tuk is certainly a part of the truth within the physical and emotional part of a puppet's many lies. Care, observation and intent are primary parts of the tuk. For example, if the puppet is looking back and forth at something stage left and then at something stage right and back to stage left to compare them, the audience might easily mistake the move as an exaggerated "no" movement. With a tuk at the end of each turn to look, the move becomes evident as a conscious and alert looking activity. In this case the tuk is almost an exclamation mark.

The tuk is also a strong element in expressing emotions through movement. In *Androcles and the Lion*, Androcles, a runaway slave, may look from side to side to see if he is being followed by the soldiers. Using the tuk in the act of looking strongly expresses his fears and nervous insecurity.

This detail may be soft or subtle, hard or obvious, or anywhere in between depending upon the performer's interpretation. In all cases be judicious in the use of new or experimental techniques. Often in learning new techniques or accents one has a tendency to overuse them ad nauseam. The trick is to use the tuk judiciously. At times a tuk can help to express and/or heighten an emotion within the puppet character. At other times the tuk will not communicate the intent. If the puppet were to look at something with a soft tuk, turn away then suddenly turn back to the same something with a hard tuk, the object becomes an emotional attraction for the character focusing on the object. The effect of the tuk in this "double take" is both physical and emotional and gold frames the move for the audience.

The tuk applied to many activities as in changing a piece of scenery the use of the tuk will tell the audience that this move is intended. Move the piece up with a small tuk, then down slowly and smoothly. The audience perceives this as an intended communicative move. Without the tuk the audience may not understand why the scenic piece suddenly went down and possibly think it to be an error.

A puppet character's standard walk may express many emotions simply by putting a tuk at the figure's foot or at the top of the head within a walking mode. Experiment, try new things ... look ... watch ... study ... and, most especially, ... think, feel and believe.

Tuck the *tuk* into the brain. Practice and discover the varieties and uses of the *tuk*.

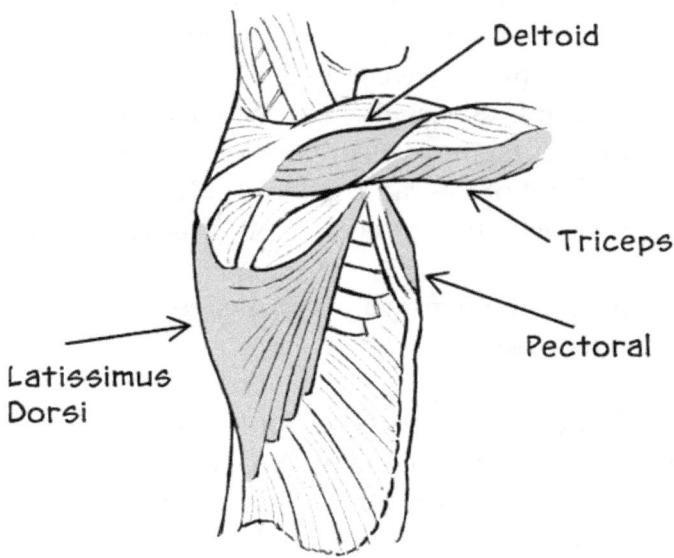

Backing Up the Arms!

Many beginning puppeteers often complain about how much their arms hurt after a very short time with the arms moving up and down in simple puppet moves. The old saw is "If it hurts, you are probably doing it right!" This *old wive's tale* is not the way it should be. Performing is not easy but it should not, necessarily, be a pain in the ... well, wherever.

The pain occurs because the performer is using the weaker deltoid and pectoral muscles of the arm, rather than the larger and stronger latissimus dorsi muscles of the back. These are strong and powerful muscles and do not tire as quickly as the deltoid and pectoral arm muscles.

The effect is similar to Tai Chi techniques to perform movement without pain. Hold the arms up in performance position, relaxed and move the back. The arms will move as the back moves. With practice, thought and care, the solar plexus muscles will give much strength and control to the puppet movements and save the suffering of pain.

The illustration shows the stance for working overhead. If working through a scrim at shoulder level, these back muscles still work far better than the weaker arm muscles. It is not what one does, in this case, it is especially how the move is accomplished. Use the latissimus dorsi muscles in packing and unpacking the equipment into and out of the car, truck or trailer. Supporting the arm moves with the back muscles is easier and far less pain.

Exercising before a performance is very useful and helpful to the puppeteer.

Some puppeteers consider the setting up and preparing the stage for performance to be exercise enough, however, the mind, body and muscles must all be consciously and physically involved in the procedure to accomplish the setup as exercise. Do not turn your back on hard work, use the latissimus dorsi muscles of the back to accomplish it with more ease and less pain.

The Hand is Quicker than the Eye!

Magician's performing sleight of hand tricks do not want the audience to see what the hands are doing and often the hands move very quickly so the audience will miss the reality and believe in the "magic" lies of the rapidly moving hands and fingers in their trickery and stunts.

The puppeteer, on the other hand, (pun intended) wants the audience to see what the arms, hands and fingers are doing to make the character expressive within the lies of truth in the art of puppet theater. It is wise to slow down (not slow motion) for the puppet actions to be clearly visible and viable.

Remember the tale of *The Tortoise and the Hare*. Slow but steady wins the race.

Plum Bob

Plumb Line & Plumb Bob

In dance, sports and other forms of physical activity, the study of movement uses a teaching technique known as the *plumb-line* or balance point. Imagine a line of cord attached beneath the center of the chin at the neck and going straight down, through the body and toward the floor with a lead weight (plumb bob) at the bottom, just between the feet. This line is the center of balance.

If the body leans forward from the ankles (not the waist) the plumb line, the balance point, goes beyond the end of the feet. The body is now off balance and one *must* move a foot forward to catch and prevent the unbalanced fall. The same is true when leaning backwards.

The same is true by leaning to either side, the plumb-line moves beyond the supporting feet and the body goes off balance and the body must adjust to maintain stability.

This *Plum Line* and *Plum Bob* idea is very important in keeping the puppet in balance and believable to the audience. For high comedic effects, the glove puppet may move *higgledy piggledy* or with heightened speed or apparent lack of control, but only when needed for the specific scene, usually highly comedic, within the play.

In today's contemporary theater, film and television, method acting is generally true to life and emotionally rich as a living reality. Puppetry is never true to life. It suggests reality, or rather, *symbolizes* a false reality by going beyond reality and into a controlled and intentional unrealistic but believable and communicative move. The moves are suggested, choreographed and rediscovered by the belief of the performer in the rediscovery of reality in the unfeasible world of glove puppetry. Again, a lie that tells the truth.

This is where the art of pretense and believability come in. Even though the puppet cannot move realistically like a human, it must reinvent and express human moves and *motives* through imaginative techniques and strongly communicative visual images, rather than attempting to depict an artificial reality. Every puppet movement is expressive and tells the audience something about the character and the situation of the moment. Keep on moving with imagination and communication working togetheras one. Anything the puppet figures says must communicate with the audience physically and emotionally, but not *simply,* orally.

4   Superstar Understudy

As said previously, the puppet is *not* the performer of the play. The puppet is a stage property in the hands of the performing puppeteer who acts out the characters, moods, intents and story of the play using the puppets to share the tale visually with the audience. The puppet begins as a blank placeholder, a Nobody, which allows the performer to freshly envision each character from scratch. This requires delving fully into the artistic process for each play, for each character, to clearly and compellingly communicate with the audience.

In puppetry, the performer is often the writer of the script, the actor playing all the characters in the play, and must often, the director. Most of the processes described here will apply.

In larger puppet productions intended for long run performances in one theater, the play is usually written by one person, directed by another, designed by yet another, created and performed by paid puppeteers in the development processes.

These larger plays and productions are happening, but require numbers of people beyond the puppeteer performers. They require directors, property managers, scenic designers, costume designers and often agents and various manners. They are happening and this is wonderful, but most puppet companies are still very limited in personnel, time and space.

Nobody as Understudy

Nobody puppets are the basic "gingerbread cookie" shaped puppet figures for developing early stages of glove puppet performance. The Nobody has no decorations of any kind: no eyes, nose nor mouths, no hair, buttons down the front, no fingers on the hands, no printed patterns on the fabric, no decorative details which may influence the puppeteer subconsciously in early learning and creating new and vital story characters.

When working with puppet types other than glove figures, it is also good to have a number of "dummy" puppets without faces, costumes or any personal features, and they should be neither male nor female, but simply blank figures. With marionettes, special strings may be added for special movements for a work in progress. The same with rod puppets, blank figures with no costumes or "character" appearance where one may add special rods or mechanics to manipulate the figure for the early rehearsals. I call all of these blank figures "Nobody" as they may play any character at any time.

The Nobody puppet is used to stimulate the performer's dramatic imagination in the early processes of puppet theater production, for learning the do's and don'ts of manipulation and in the preliminary rehearsals, discovering the needs, quality and form in the creation of a new play.

Positioning the Nobody Glove Puppet

Trident Position: The performer puts the Nobody on the hand in the Trident position which I think is the most efficient and my strongly recommended hand position. Place the pointer finger and long finger together in the head pushing up into the center of the stuff-

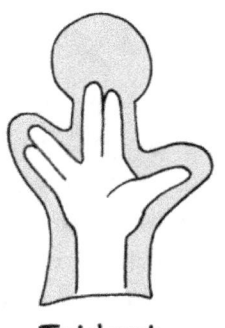

Trident

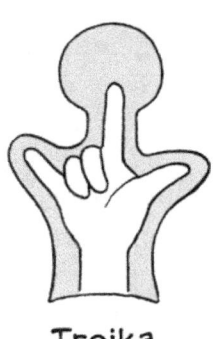

Troika

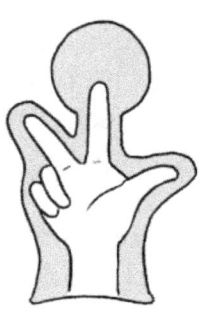

Treble

ing. The thumb fits into one arm and the ring and little fingers together in the other arm. The lower body hem is at or below the elbow. The *Trident* position is very flexible and the most fluid position for the hand to manipulate the figure with ease and flexibility. It is also the strongest and best for handling puppet props which glove puppets use with great skill. The *Trident* position can do almost anything a glove puppet may need to accomplish.

Troika: The *Troika* is another format for creating a more realistic look. While I do not advise this position, it is used by many puppeteers. The pointer finger goes into the head, the thumb into one arm and the little finger into the other arm. The two other fingers fold down into the "chest" of the figure. This position works for some characters and for special subtle theatrical and poetic moves requiring more fluid, richer or elegant full figured appearance. It does have some special qualities but the puppet head cannot turn from side to side for looking, for negative head moves or for whatever needs a turning head.

Trebel: The *Treble* position should be called the *Trouble* position! It is the easiest position for the untrained hands of beginners. It is also the least effective and most awkward of all the many possible hand positions. The head cannot be turned from side to side It is very weak for handling properties and is clumsy for expressions of emotions. The troubled *Treble* is *strongly advised against!* If a puppeteer uses this position, it is a bad habit. *Break the habit!*

I strongly recommend the *Trident* position for all, or at least, most glove puppet figures.

Other Positions: In many old folktales animals act, move, talk and think like humans rather than animals. Many of these tales are, intentionally, comically mocking human behavior but using animals to soften the mockery. The *Uncle Remus Tales* featuring Br'er Rabbit, Br'er Fox and Br'er Bear are fine examples of that motif as are many Native American tales and some Victorian classic tales. The puppeteer's hand positions are the same as for human characters.

In many other plays, animals like dogs, cats, hippopotami, elephants, monsters, or other imaginatively designed creatures, may need special hand positions or mechanical controls to be worked out individually to fill the specific performance needs.

Plays or stories calling for crazy *critters* with wheels, multiple heads, tentacles, or whatever the creator's imagination demands, may also require individual hand positions, puppet types, or mechanical inner workings for fine and meaningful manipulation.

Movement Speaks Louder than Words

Audiences go to *hear* a lecture, a concert or a speech. They go to *see* a ballet, a movie, a play or a puppet performance. In Shakespeare's time puppets were referred to as *motions*, and in modern day Europe, puppetry is often referred to as *animation*. Puppetry is a strongly visual art form and the motions and physical actions expressing ideas and emotions are far more effective than speech alone.

This does not mean dialogue is unimportant or should not be used, but rather that movement is the primary function in glove puppet performances, dialogue supports and underscores the motivations of the character at any moment within the play. Dialogue may support, enhance and, at times, clarify the movement.

Glove puppets cannot look or move like humans. The puppeteer must reinvent a normal walk by *faking* the idea. These odd glove puppet figures can, however, strongly suggest the human conditions emotionally, dramatically and communicatively through well choreographed movement, blended with speech as needed by the play itself. The Nobody often comes to life as understudy for the finished figures.

For marionettes, mitt puppets, rod puppets, shadow figures and other puppet styles, it is wise to have characterless figures for practice, teaching and early rehearsals in developing new productions. The movements for these other puppet types must also be plotted and planned to accomplish the various mechanical needs of the form used. Special strings, rods or other mechanisms may be needed to express a character.

Rehearsal Formats

Planning a play for short run performances as in schools, libraries, art galleries or museums is quite different from planning a production to (hopefully) be performed for a long run of possibly several weeks, months or even years in a permanent professional situation similar to a touring musical comedy after a Broadway success.

Short run plays use portable stages, scenery or a decorative format to be set up relatively quickly, the performances are offered on the same day, and the performer repacks the equipment back into the vehicle and rides to the next performance.

For a longer range performances in professional theaters that may run for several weeks, or even months, the scenery and performing equipment is more complex and is usually set up by professional backstage crews. The performers rehearse the show on stage for the lighting and any sound equipment or live orchestra needed for performance. The performance then, hopefully runs successfully for a longer run of weeks or months.

Aladdin and His Wonderful Lamp

5 Let the Fingers Do the Talking

Not surprisingly the hands are key to manipulating any style of puppet figure so it clearly communicates with the audience. The following techniques were originally created by Carol Fijan, of the National Theater of Puppet Arts in New York, and were partially inspired by Stanislavsky's *System,* now widely known as *Method Acting*, which is very different for a puppeteer and a puppet object than for human actors.

Variations in techniques will be needed for different styles of puppets.

In glove puppetry, these moves are classic and enhance communication with an audience of any age. The performer's fingers, wrists and arms are used in carefully plotted moves to express, explain and communicate strongly with the audience, with or without the words and not an imitation of human moves, but rather moves expressing *human emotions* through the gestures.

Other puppet forms will need special strings or mechanisms to accomplish some of the moves, but the concept of expressing the emotions through movement is applicable to all puppet forms.

The glove puppet moves described below use the fingers of the performer's hands.

Play with the various moves, but do not become glued to them. They are all suggestions and possibilities. Use the brain and avoid over-use of any one movement. There are a great number of fine and telling moves a puppet may use that are not expressed here.

Experiment, communicate, try new things and discover what works for both the performers and the audiences!

Basic Stance

The puppet stands with its hands lightly touching in front of the body. The pose is basic and simple. Most hand and body moves begin in this position, do what they need to do and usually return to the same basic pose. No one stands with their arms stretched out and up in the air. Nor should a puppet.

The glove puppet, unfortunately, cannot have its hands hang down by the sides. Therefore the basic stance is the puppet's picture image of standing relaxed, still, tall and straight, not a pretensive attempt to duplicate true to living human movements.

Finger Moves

Yes: The Nobody puppet stands in the prime position, hands touching in front. Nod the head two or three times by bending the two fingers in the neck. The puppet easily expresses *"yes"* without speaking.

The nod expresses many dynamics within the meaning of "Yes." A single Nod done very slowly might suggest doubt or insecurity or *"yes?"* as a question. Nodding more strongly suggests anger or insistence! Nodding quickly may be an eager agreement, or the delight of an idea expressed. Experiment with the emotional dynamics, strengths and speeds of the *yes* nod, add vocal agreements.

Express the final, cannot be denied single nod: *Yes!* The argument is over! Experiment with *Yes* movements without words. Emotional *motivations* of the character affect the *dynamics* of all dialogue and moves.

Movement and Dialogue: Even though glove puppet mouths do not move, nodding the head is never used to show the audience the puppet is talking. Most humans do not talk by bobbing their heads up and down like chickens pecking in the dirt, nor should a puppet. It means nothing to the audience, and inhibits other attempts to communicate. With two or more puppets on stage, it is the speaker who moves and gestures to express their motivations. It is clear which puppet is doing the talking. Other figures listen without moving except with an *occasional* emotional agreement, disagreement or other reaction to the speaker's dialogue.

Movement vs. Dialogue: Dialogue is *supplemental* to the movement. Not the other way around. As has been said, one goes to *see* a puppet play, not to *hear* it. Keep that thought and intent actively in mind.

There are *always* exceptions to every idea or suggestion. *Usually* the listeners just listen and respond a bit to what they hear. The listening figure must not move so much that it distracts from the speaker *unless* the character is *intentionally upstaging* the speaker for comic affect. Comic speechmakers often speak foolishly almost without breathing while the other character(s) might do anything that is ridiculous and overshadowing of the speaker's yakking.

No: The head turns from side to side by twisting the two fingers within the head and neck in expressing No. There may be times when the whole body turns to express No! Especially when it needs to be strong, or in a large performance hall where a smaller movement might not be seen. Each may be used depending on meaning, need and emotions within the play. Experiment with "No!" Play with it. Shaking the head "No" can be calm, angry, dramatic or strong and emphatic. An emotionally intense "No!" might be done by slapping the hand down on a table, stomping a foot (not easy for a glove puppet but easy to fake by moving the costume like a knee move). Turning the character's back on the other character. Jumping up and down in a fury of No! No! No! Movement is controlled by the emotions behind the words, the motivation, not by the words alone.

Move with the emotions and motivations of the character rather than the words alone.

Self: These moves are self-recognition, a fine character expression. The puppet points to itself once and the puppet may be saying; "My name is ..." or "Are you talking about *me*?" For stronger emphasis the puppet may vary the intensity and intent of the moves and words, "I am the best that I can be!" or "I am the smartest man in Siam! *Yes*, I am!"

Touching the self may express *ego* and may be done strongly, modestly or with other movements expressing *me* and *I* depending on the personality and motivation. Self moves may be used as a modest personal acknowledgement, for pompous *braggadocio* or however the *me* is expressive of the character at that moment in the play.

Pointing: The puppet points in a direction. "Please put that chair over *there*.", "No, no, try it over *here*!", "No! That looks too isolated. Let's try it on *that* side." The puppet may look either in the direction of the point, or at the character handling the chair, or from one to the other, as needed.

Focus is essential at all times on stage, whether the performer is using a faceless Nobody or a figure with fully sculpted and painted facial features. The puppet may point up, down, and point to things in the area around it, and the eyes follow the point. A character's gaze absolutely *never* stares off into empty space as it points, talks or waits. The performer must always be conscious of where and why the puppet is looking.

Point the puppet's *nose* at the visual object and the audience will read it as visual looking.

Waving: Waving is often used to attract attention "Hey, you, I'm over here!" or as a welcoming, "Hello!" or a parting "Good bye." Waving in welcome or other positive reasons is best done with the puppeteer's ring and little finger. It may be done quickly or slowly depending on the intent and motivation.

The character would wave differently if the recipient is nearby or at a distance. A rapid waving suggests, "Hello! Welcome! I'm so glad to see you!" A slower movement, with the thumb, is more like "Good bye. We'll miss you." Waving still more sadly, "We'll miss you! Keep in touch! Goodbye!" The puppet waves sadly as the scenic train pulls away on its imaginary journey. The meaning of the wave depends upon the motivations of the characters, "I'll see you around, bye!" could be meaningful in a positive or a negative way. The sound of the voice and texture of the wave will be very expressive. The intent and/or meaning within the script and the performer's interpretation of the lines and the character's motivation.

Come Here: An urging with the thumb, or a broader move of the ring finger and the pinkie is a broader gesture, "Come over here!" The puppet's arm moves with the gesture in an arc with a side to side movement of the wrist in stronger excitement. "Come! Look what I just found!", or a similar gesture of urgency, "Hurry up! We'll be late!" For a less exuberant move, the puppet may simply move the hand in a smaller, slower move. The puppet's eyes may be focused on the item of interest, or person spoken to. Doing the same move more rapidly and powerfully for an urgent "Come on, we have to go!" or "Hurry up!" or angrily, "Git yer friggin' butt over here!"

Rubbing the Hands: The puppet may rub its hands in many different ways, agitated, slowly, swiftly, broadly. "I'm c-c-c-cold.", "Heh, heh, heh! You *must* pay the rent!" and "All right now ... let's get to work!" and *Lady Macbeth's* distress in her sleepwalking scene: "Out, out damned spot! Out I say! Here's the smell of the blood still. All the perfumes of Arabia will not sweeten this little hand." Each time she rubs her hands it must be a different mood of guilt, desperation, fear, complicity, sorrow, and even happiness, each with a different degree of agitation or inner emotion. Rubbing the hands together will be expressive of the puppet character's intent in the moment.

Thinking: There are many ways to express the character is thinking, planning, plotting or conniving, and more. It is important to play with all major ideas visually as well as vocally.

Thinking movements depend on the *inner* meaning of the move. What is being thought? What is the character's inner, unspoken feeling about that thought? How might the thoughts be expressed without words? Might they be better expressed through movement and words combined? It depends upon the script and the situation within the play.

If spoken, what is the intended effect on the audience? If expressed by a movement, is the emotion a deeper or stronger expression of the inner needs of the character?

Movement without words is powerful. Movement and words together are also strong. Tapping the head, "Now where is that *book*?" Throwing up the arms, "Now *where* is that book?" Rubbing the chin "Now where *is* that book?" or a frustrated, "*Now* where is that book? It was here just a minute ago!"

Self Touching: A puppet should be able to touch various parts of itself, expressively but not naughtily.

Well, okay, sometimes naughtily if it is important within the scene! The puppet may scratch an itch, rub an ache, push back a lock of hair, smooth a skirt. How and *why* might a puppet stroke a beard, curl a mustache, blow a kiss, wipe away a tear, brush lint from a shirt sleeve or straighten a tie, or almost any small but meaningful activity?.

How might a Nobody puppet with no mouth and no fingers express a small child sucking its thumb? The *sound* of sucking and the movement of the head will sell the idea to the audience.

Wipe a tear from the eye, touch the heart, rub the stomach, rub the forehead, cover the ears, cover the eyes, touch the nose. The sweet coquette fluffs her hair flirtatiously while the young swain stands a bit taller adjusting his already perfect tie. A puppet might brush off a sleeve. A *guy* dating his *gal* would brush differently than a *Renaissance Doge* brushing his embroidered silken sleeve for emphatic show before rendering a death sentence. It is not a question of *what* the puppet is doing, it is the *why* and *how* the *character* functions that inspires the puppet moves.

Crawling: The puppet figure goes down on the play board and crawls forward on its hands. Is the crawling character a baby, a mouse, or a cat? Is it an adult crawling because it is injured and cannot walk, or a person crawling sneakily toward some desired wicked goal? How might a snake slither, a spider scuttle, a human sneak on hands and knees? A cat crawls differently from a squirrel on the ground. Keep the puppet's head up as it crawls, the audience wants and needs to see the face in a final performance.

Crawl (walk) like a turtle, like a scampering mouse. Play with the idea of crawling, make it cute, menacing, desperate or hopeful. An old miner or pioneer crawling through the desert without water. The puppet would need to look up occasionally to see where he is going, to see the mirage of a shade tree and a lake in the distance. Perhaps, to see there is no place or reason to go on. What happens next in this tale of woe?

Creeping: Creeping is a "puppet only" move. The puppet goes down, with its two hands together on the play board and facing front with the head held up high, then stretch a hand out to the side with an exaggerated arc-shaped move and down on the play board, and bring the other hand together with the first in a similar arc. Repeating enough to cover the specific space. Creeping is a movement similar to tiptoeing, and like tiptoeing, the move may be done sneakily, playfully or as if frightened, fast or slow or however needed in a scene. How and when a move is used depends on the needs of the character and its needs within the play.

New & Inventive Moves: There are many movements for the puppet's head, arms and body. Experiment with new movements to express ideas and emotions not covered here. Plan out the movement of a puppet's arms when it is singing a solo in recital. Singing a rock song is much different from singing a love serenade, or a song and dance routine in a musical comedy from an operatic aria sung either seriously or for comic affect. These simple but expressive movements are only a few of the many possibilities. Create your own puppet movements to express the characters and the situ ations they are in. Words need movement. Movement does not, necessarily, need words, but certainly emotional motivation will determine the details.

Classical Tales

6   A Twist of the Wrist

As a puppeteer begins to craft the Nobody's larger, upper body movements, the same principles apply: the meaning dictates the movement; there are many ways to do any action and how it's done matters in communicating with the audience.

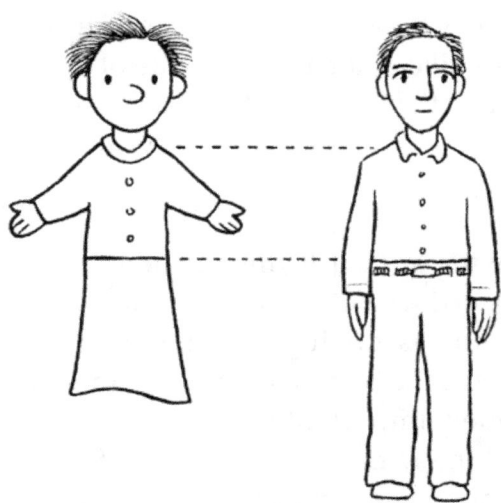

The wrist acts as the Nobody's waist in the front and the rear end in the back. The palm of the hand is the puppet's solar plexus and the source of breath and breathing. (The human solar plexus is physically located below the waist in the lower abdomen with the diaphragm.) Unfortunately a glove puppet has no lower abs. The hand within the puppet cannot breathe or expand below the wrist. Breathing is suggested by expanding the palm in a small move and slightly bending the wrist back. The illusion is very like taking in a small breath of fresh air. Have the puppet breathe gently, more robustly and very heavily. Play with breathing, experiment, find different ways to inhale and exhale with the puppet. How many different emotions can be expressed just by breathing?

Bending Over

Bending over from the waist is simple and obvious. The important thing is attitude. Why is the figure bending over? Something on the ground attracts the character's notice? There is a hole in the ground and the figure wonders about it? To smell a flower? To tie a shoe lace? The puppet is looking for something in the grass or sees something in the grass that he or she is curious about and wants to pick up? A diamond ring, a piece of paper with writing on it, a pirate's treasure map, a beautiful flower, something disgusting and nasty like a dead rat or a pile of dog pooh! What is it? How important is it" How does the character feel about whatever it is?

Bowing

Bowing and curtsying are no longer forms of recognition in the western world. Younger audience members might mistake the bowing as looking for something and a simple nod of the head may replace the bow or curtsy in a modern performance. If a bow is extremely important to the dramatic needs of a classic scene, it must be done with a strong degree of regality. The bow must be choreographed to *sell* the idea to the audience.

To bow effectively, the puppet spreads one or both arms stretching out wide. The figure slowly bends at the waist, keeping the back straight and the head up, looking at the recipient of the bow. The figure stands up, tall and straight, the speed of which is determined by the *attitude* and *intent* of the character.

Any grand personage from the Middle Ages to the Victorian era in a play, might bow excessively grandly when appropriate. They might put one hand to the waist, the other arm widely outstretched and, again, the figure bends from the waist, keeping the back straight and the head up, eyes on the recipient. Then rising to full height, and bringing the arm down with a flair.

The recipient of the bow must respond in some way, a simple nod of acceptance, break into laughter, acknowledge the bow with a simple nod or respond with a threat. A poor and humble man would bow quite differently from a diplomat. He might show his fear and discomfort at being before the King. Bowing may be done humbly, coldly, politely, or sharply in contempt, or fearfully or what is needed for the character and the story.

Shrugging

A glove puppet cannot shrug in a realistic way, but it can be *suggested*! The puppet's arms move up and out from the basic stance, the puppet body leans a little at the waist and a tilt of the head to the side with a fairly substantial tuk.

"Those things just happen!" "I don't know. It could be anywhere." "Who cares?" "Whacha gonna do?" or "Why should I care?" A wise guy, a cool desperado or scoundrel might tilt the head sideways quickly shrug from the puppeteer's wrist with an "Eh?" sound.

Sitting Down & Standing Up

A glove puppet cannot sit on a realistic prop chair with a seat. The puppeteer's arm does not bend in the right places for the act of sitting to occur easily. It must be plotted out and choreographed for seeming reality. However, the glove puppet may easily sit down on the stage playboard.

1. The Nobody leans forward from the waist.
2. The Nobody is lowered to the playboard still leaning.
3. Nobody straightens up, sitting comfortably or uncomfortably, as needed dramatically.

The act of getting up from sitting is the same three count move in reverse.

1. The Nobody leans forward.
2. Nobody, still leaning forward, rises from the chair by lifting the butt up.
3. Nobody then stands up as tall and straight as usual.

A glove puppet with no legs or knees to bend cannot easily sit on a prop chair. One technique is for the puppet to sit on the chair with the back to the audience. The knee-less sit will not be seen, but if properly done, will be believed. The set designer must *create* a chair on which a glove puppet can sit while allowing for the puppeteer's unyielding arm. A chair might be built with arms and a back with a painted image or faked with a very shallow seat for the puppet to *appear* to sit down on. Once seated the puppet must be kept at the same faked level of a nonexistent seat, which is the hard part.

The move, depending on the character, may be done smoothly, staggered roughly, cleanly or varied in many ways depending on the *intent* of the move ... the *motivation*! The character's mood and intent will also affect everything the character does. An elegant grand dame might sit with great dignity on the playboard or a mock chair, lowering herself elegantly into a sitting pose and a brushing with a hand to smooth her dress.

Another elderly character might lower him or herself slowly down and perhaps plop down into the sitting position at the end of the move, and rise with an extra heavy push up to a standing position. A very obese figure would just sort of drop heavily into the seat, getting up would be showing a heavy push upward. A slim and agile teenager might not sit in a chair, but drape the body over the chair. How might a bum, a drunkard or person with sore feet sit? Most people would follow the one, two three steps above but with added emotional reason – happy, sad, lonely or thinking of something with an emotional edge to it.

In a play situation, the puppet's physical, emotional and character attitudes will affect everything. Emotions, character and moods can be easily shown or suggested within any of these moves: angrily, sadly, happily, grandly, carelessly, with great dignity, disgruntled or with a giggle of delight or whatever is called for in the script or emotions of the scene.

Worrying

How does one show worry? It begins with the classic *Who, Why, What, When* and *How*? *Who* is the character? *Why* is he or she worried? *What* is/are the character(s) worried about? *When* did it happen? *How* serious are the consequences of the worry? Is the action theatrically meaningful, comedic, adventurous, classic or tragic in style?

A character's hands may go to the sides of the head and the figure sway from side to side. Take a deep breath and sigh heavily. Bang the head against a tree, a door or wall. Pace back and forth to easily express mood and worry. A worried mother looking for a lost child in a department store would move in very different ways than the lost child looking for the safety of Mama's loving arms.

The Mother in *"Hansel and Gretel"* sends the children into the woods to gather berries for dinner. She might nervously go to the window several times to see if the two children are returning home to ease her own fears and guilt about sending the children out into the dark woods.

There are so many possible *"worry"* movements, which may be needed in the demands of a play, that it would be impossible to list them all. The performer must interpret the character, the What and Why of the worry to express the emotion within the needs of the play. Is the worry sincere or insincere? Is it strong or casual? Who? What? Why? How?

Yawning & Stretching

There are as many ways to yawn as there are to worry. Glove puppet magic is essential.

If one is to inhale or exhale a breath while patting the mouth with the hand, a polite move, (that also covers the fact the puppet mouth does not open). The big yawn is to stretch the arms out wide, rock from side to side, with loud heavy inhaled and exhaled sounds of breaths or appropriate sounds. Then the figure collapses the lungs with a hearty exhaling sigh.

A very polite character might begin a yawn, then quickly pat the lips with the hand to cover the unintended expression of tiredness or boredom. The stronger yawn might be a broad stretch of the arms, reaching out as far as the fingers can stretch with a swaying movement from side to side, then the collapse of the arms and the tension on the outgoing breath.

It could be a stretch before or after a good sleep, or to get the body to moving after sitting too long. It might be slight boredom to major boredom in many different story needs. Why does one stretch? What yawning sounds are appropriate? When is one likely to stretch? Stretch the imagination, too. Why is the character yawning? How does the character feel about it? How important is it in that moment of the play? How might other characters respond to the yawning?

Noisy Movements?

There are many puppet moves that *need* the sounds to make them understandable. Most of these are natural body functions: laughing, crying, hiccuping, yawning, coughing, breathing, gasping, belching, farting, retching, snoring, sneezing, chewing, gulping, sniffling and an unimaginable number of them that could show up, or rather, *sound* up.

The moves related to these sounds are not strong or varied enough for the audience to comprehend without the natural accompanying sounds. This is one of the few places where sound is as important as the movement. Yelps of "OOF!", "Ouch!" and any vocal sounds from a fall to the floor are also needed, even in a non-vocal acting scene. A butt from any one of the Billy Goats Gruff would cause the troll to make a sound.

All of them may be done in different ways and degrees depending on whether it is to be simply expressive, lightly humorous or highly comedic, moody, obviously vulgar or simply expressing a character or situation at the moment with or without dialogue.

Folk Tales from Japan

7 Puppets Up in Arms

The arms of the puppeteer create the puppet's body moves. Begin with the Nobody puppet standing up straight and tall, in the basic stance. From the basic stance the puppet may walk, run, dance, fist fight, wrestle, wallow on the ground or whatever the script devises for the tale being told. Since the glove puppet has no legs, it is necessary to invent actions that suggest walking, running, jumping, dancing and any important body moves, in ways which convey the actions of the legless motions of the character to the audience.

Walking

No two puppet characters should walk in the same exact style. Each individual has personal characteristics, emotions and "habits" which may affect the walking moves. Occasionally a child will walk imitating their same sex parent, but that is the actor's choice of interpretation.

Experiment by using the *tuk* at the beginning or ending of a walk move for expressing mood and stronger meaning. Learn from it, rediscover the reality of the artificial moves to reinvent the act of walking without legs.

Walk the figure across the room in the air for practice and cross the space for a few yards. If the puppet must walk a distance on or off the stage, the puppeteer must walk with the puppet. Not only will the puppeteer's walk affect the puppets movements, the puppet will usually appear to be more alive. Watch the puppet carefully, do not let it sag, lean over or sink into the imagined walkway beneath it. Keep it light and simple, and pay full attention to every move and variation. Here are some walking techniques to build from.

Peak & Vale: Variations of this technique are the most often used by glove puppeteers around the world, however, do not allow it to become a habit.

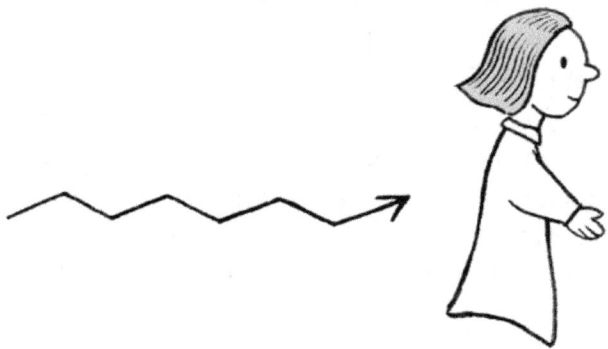

Every character is different and will walk with individual variations within the technique.

Simply move the puppet up about two inches as it goes forward and down again as it continues, and repeating the Peak & Vale move as the figure walks forward in this simple up and forward and down and forward move. Perform the moves again, but this time add emotional variations.

Show the figure is happy, angry, sad, worried, overjoyed or physically or emotionally stressed. This calls for the *tuk* either at the crest of the peak or the bottom of the vale for emphasis, or both if needed or wanted.

Arch: The figure stands up straight and tall and walks by moving forward in a slight curved arch up and down and repeated as the character moves across the space. The move is repeated as the figure walks across the space with each "step". The size of the arch may be varied for different moods, different characters and different needs of communication with the audiences of the future.

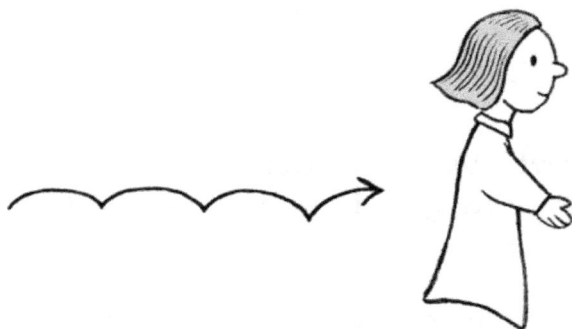

Experiment with this *Arch* walk. Make the arch wider, higher, faster, slower. Accent with a tuk and or a slight pause at the lower points. Watch the move, study the puppet and observe the move and think about what the puppet is doing, feeling or sharing.

Dip: The *dip* is the *arch* in reverse, the figure goes down and curves the dip with an upward move in an inverted arch up to the floor of the playboard. Repeat this downward dip, watching for mood and intent of the character. Note how this alters the character's mood. Play with adding a *tuk* at the top of the "*up*" peak of the *Dip*. Play with the various moods of the puppet in action, different speeds and minor details.

Again, play with adding the *tuk* in the walking at the feet, the head or both at once.

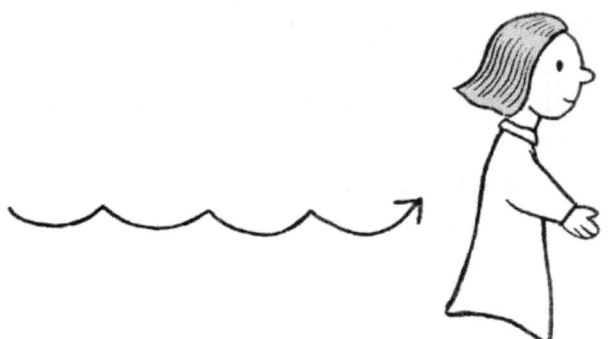

Arch & Dip: The arch and dip moves may be combined into one walking style. Think of it as an "S" lying down on its back. The figure moves in a small arch followed by a small dip.

By simply performing these moves one after the other in a smooth walk across the puppet playboard, one has created a believable character style. Walk the Nobody across the playboard for practice. Make sure the puppet is standing tall and erect all across the pretend playboard. What emotions can the character convey?

Twist: Instead of moving the figure up and down, the figure turns from side to side at each *step*. Walk the puppet along for a bit. The human elbow simply slides forward as the puppet body turns from left to right. Now walk the figure with just a twist of the head by moving the fingers in the neck.

There are many variations of slow to fast, fast to slow, fast to a dead stop and many fun and interesting variations. Play with all these moves to find what works best and most affectively for the puppet character in action.

Tic-Tock: For this move the puppet, standing straight and tall, walks the across the stage, swaying like a metronome or an upside down clock pendulum from the elbow as the puppet moves forward across the stage or space. Vary the degree and the speed of swaying. Add the tuk at each side of the move. A different character might cross by swaying from the puppeteer's wrist rather than the elbow. The elbow would "glide" along as the upper body of the puppet moves from side to side. Now one might vary the move by swaying just the head from side to side. Add the tuk at various places in these moves, watching, judging, experimenting with variations in each walk.

Swinger: The figure walks by keeping the head over the elbow, moving the wrist from side to side. This walk suggests a woman walking with swaying hips. Might a male figure walk with his hips moving? Certainly the affect and technique could be different. Play with it by exaggerating or minimizing the movement and do not neglect the sexual innuendo possibilities. Move the figure's *hips* in a circle. Also add the tuk to the move, experiment, invent, discover and vary the character and personality in the Nobody. Invent moves for a puppet to show a swagger, a stagger, a foot stomper (without feet) or other walk techniques to discover.

Zigzag: The zigzag begins by standing the puppet up straight and tall. Then, keeping the head (Puppeteer's fingers) and the feet (puppeteer's elbow) in place, move the puppet's butt (wrist) back and then forward beyond the *feet* (elbow).

Move the figure's head and feet forward beyond the puppeteer's wrist and then the puppet's waist (the wrist) moves forward while the head and feet (fingers and elbow) remain in place, wrist moves forward beyond the fingers and elbow, then remains still as the fingers and elbow move forward beyond the waist (the wrist). Play with one's own hand to discover other walks one might use for a puppet in a scene. Find humorous moves for comic characters and less comedic moves for more normal characters.

Stroke & Scoop: Play with the *stroke* and *scoop* moves vertically for a character walking across the stage. Vary the dynamics of these two moves to find what works as character walks, with varying moods and intents. The *scoop* move can be elegant, humorous, angry or comical depending on how it is done. Play with it. Experiment with the *stroke* move to find its many variations.

Elegant Walk: The elegant walk is similar to a bride walking down the aisle or a monarch at their coronation into royal office. A slow and graceful "*dip*" move or perhaps just a short slide forward and stop, again slide forward and stop. Elegant moves might be done with subtle variations of the scoop and stroke moves, or perhaps a simple slide forward and a soft stop and another simple slide and soft stop until the figure has reached the intended goal. Experiment and invent new and different aspects of walking elegantly and for some dignified intent.

Running: As a broad generality, most characters will run in the same move as they walk, but with more speed and energy expended and usually leaning forward a little or very much atilt.

One big exception is the Elegant Walk. It is impossible to run elegantly because *elegance* is a practiced quality. One cannot run elegantly, especially when fleeing from a threatening or frightening situation. Play, invent, create and let the imagination walk, run and gallop. Other moves of dramatic expression are important to work on: experiment, play, discover, invent and reinvent. All walks and runs are performed with a puppet without legs to walk on, more lies that tell the truth.

Other Walks: Invent a walk for an old bowlegged cowboy, a very elderly person with or without a cane, a drunken character or a different move for someone feeling sick. Move a clown, a robot, or whatever the mind may conjure up for other personalities walking. An enormously obese person, obviously, will walk differently from a thin and agile individual.

Limping

Pain in one foot, knee or leg, causes the limp. Usually it's a single pain but occasionally several at once. Practice walking as if one's own foot hurts sharply (right or left). Each time the foot steps down there is pain, so the figure quickly steps off the sore foot and puts the pressure on the foot that does not hurt. Then, slowly, the figure steps, again, on the hurt foot. The process is repeated painful step after painful step, until one has limped away. Limp the figure across the stage (perhaps using the "foot" closest to the audience as the sore one in order for them to better "see" the limp).

Experiment with the tuk, with various soft and hard uses. Different locales of the pain such as back pain or knee pain would be different from a sprained ankle or sore foot. Experiment with different ways for the figure to limp. Exaggerate for humor or for drama.

Falling & Fainting

When a puppet trips and falls, it first lifts slightly up, struggles to catch its balance, and then falls down. The fall down is better if done a bit slower than reality.

Meryl Oberon, in the black and white film, *The Scarlet Pimpernel*, wearing an elegant and wide hoop skirted costume, fainted. She went down slowly and gracefully, her skirt billowing out beautifully around her. She fell into a graceful pose on the floor in a very lovely old-fashioned faint. Try that using a Nobody puppet with a full skirt affixed for the needs of the movement.

The puppet is now lying down on the play board. How does the lovely damsel in a hoop skirt rise from this fall or faint? Does another character offer her smelling salts? Assist in her rising? Does the handsome hero lift the fainted figure up and carry her to a comfortable settee to fully recover from the loss of breath? Old movies are a great learning experiences?

How might a cowboy, an elderly person or any character rise from a fall, faint, magic spell or for any other reason? The various characters and reasons for the fall will require responses to differ in expressing the effects of a fall.

There are times when a puppet in a severe fall needs to thump down onto the playboard, usually making a good loud noise. Audiences love a good hard fall! However, do not *thump* it! *Fake* it. Do not crush the puppet's head, knock over the stage or break the puppeteer's hand in the process of creating the illusion of a hard fall!

The puppeteer's free hand might slap the play board, prop shelf or one might stomp a foot on the floor for the noise of the fall, a recorded sound track also works well but the timing must be absolutely exact. A brief musical or other sound cue before the "thump" creates a good aid for timing. Disconnected sound cues and actions are highly amateurish.

Each of these variations will take some practice to do well, but can save bruised hands, dented puppet heads, implement the lies and still be strongly communicative to the audience, which is the intent of all of this theatrical fakery.

When a puppet falls down and does not bounce, children will often assume the puppet character is dead. "That puppet is dead!" a five year old will say. When the figure bounces lightly on hitting the stage, it is perceived to be alive. Once the fallen puppet is lying on the ground, awake or unconscious, it must continue to visually breathe, moving softly as needed for effect.

Jumping, Hopping & Leaping

Jumping, perhaps reaching for something in a high place, the puppet does not simply go up into the air to pluck an object too far away to reach. It goes down first, as if bending the knees, (visualize) then pushes off in a fast jump, with some effort. It slows a bit as it reaches the peak of the jump, pauses for a tiny fraction of a second, the hands trying to reach the coveted object, then drops back down to the ground with a "bending" at the impact before standing up to full height. Any of these jumping bits may be done slower than reality so the audience can see it, or in a manner that will communicate to the audience for fact, fun or fallacy.

Hopping an animal puppet, perhaps a rabbit, would require a slight downward move and then a faster and more vital push off. After the hop up (and a slight pause in mid air) it alights and lands without a bump at the bottom. The puppet hopping is not the way a living rabbit hops, but suggestive of it. The puppeteer must *create* moves to make the audience believe the action. A slightly exaggerated or designed move is often stronger than the realistic move. Fakery is often the golden touch revealing the truth within a puppet play!

Dancing, Fighting & High Action Choreography

Glove puppets can dance very well, but need to be well planned and *choreographed*. Puppets jiggling up and down in time to the music is not expressive of dancing. It is simply poor manipulation. Since glove puppets seldom have legs on which to dance, it must dance in sways and turns with dance-like head, body and arm moves, sometimes flowing with the music and sometimes contrary to the music. If one has no strong dance knowledge or experience, find someone with dance skills to help. What kind of dance is the character doing and why? An elderly puppet dreamily dancing alone in the remembrance of a long ago event? Two figures doing a folk or traditional dance as a variety piece or as an appropriate part of a play?

Any physically or emotionally active move must be worked out in detail for the audience to feel and sense it. Every major move must be designed to be visibly accurate and interesting in a way the audience can *read* it and *perceive* what is happening. The audience should be drawn into the emotions through the movement.

The same principals would be true of a dream, a fist fight, a jolly song, an angry argument between two puppets, or any intense and highly important physical actions need to be carefully worked or choreographed and rehearsed to perfection within the play. Paul Zaloom, a fine puppeteer, once created a scene in which two characters had a brawling fist fight at vibrant fighting speed, and then repeated the very same fight in slow motion for the audience to really see what happened. It was a delight for all. The choreography of the fight was exact in detail in both the fast and slow versions, except the fast version was so fast it was impossible to see the individual movements of the puppets, only that they were fighting at great speed. The slower speed showed the moves were precise, accurate and very comical to see the figures fighting in slow motion.

If the fight is a major scene in a drama, it must be accomplished just slowly enough for the audience to see, feel and care about the event without realizing it is slower than reality!

Sleeping

Just as sitting, standing and walking are a challenge for the anatomy of the glove puppet, so is sleeping. Like all moves, *Sleeping* is based on and shaped by character, script and story needs. The character sits on the play board (or bed), yawns and stretches. A puppet prop bed might have a blanket on it. The puppet lifts the blanket, sits on the bed, lies down and pulls the blanket up over itself. The affect is joyful and interesting to the audience, not knowing how much invention creative imagination occurs backstage to make the scene believable.

The Nobody lies down and perhaps shifts positions trying to be comfortable. If there is a pillow, the puppet may poke and/or adjust the pillow, place and replace the pillow and lean down on it, fuss with it and finally settle down for a long winter's or summer's night.

A puppet with eyes painted or sculptured open, might be made to lie down and then roll over, turning its back to the audience who willingly believe the figure is falling into a sleep with the proper breathing and sleeping moves. The palm of the hand inside the puppet is its source of breath and will slowly open and close in rhythmic breathing movements. Now the puppet sleeps, per chance to dream. Aye there's the rub! For in that pretense of sleep, what scripted dreams may issue from a creative puppeteer's imagination?

How might the puppeteer create a dream "balloon" over the sleeping puppet? A puppet in a nightmare would move and breathe differently from a beautiful or pleasant dream, a lusty dream, or simply a deep sleep. All depends entirely on the character's personality, the situation within the story and the script and what the performer wants the audience to know.

A rough or comic character might snore, an elegant character may or may not. Reactions on awakening from a dreadful nightmare or a lovely sentimental dream need to be well plotted and rendered artistically with powerful affect to communicate the true idea to the audience.

Young Couple from
A Musical Variety Show

8 Nobody Becomes a Who

Every character has gender, age and a name. Each character is physical, mental, emotional and social. These elements are created and controlled by the intent of the writer of the play, the characterization and content of the play, the inspiration of the director, the interpretation of the performer, and by the age of the intended audience. Each element of this identity and its portal must be carefully thought through so it may be fully communicated to the audience.

Character Development

Gender: Obviously everyone has gender. In most puppet theater, especially for children, the gender of the character is either female or male.

In adult works, gender and sexuality could include gay, transgender, cross dressers or of no specific gender. In science fiction the gender could be whatever the creative imagination may conceive. In puppet theater one may magnify the good old imagination to the farthest extent so long as it is appropriate for the intended audience.

Age: Behavior and physical activity is more important to an audience than the specific age. The actor playing the role must know (or choose) everything about a character in creating that character believably. Little Red Riding Hood at three years of age will not think, act or behave in the same way at six, or ten and will vary greatly at sixteen or twenty. In the original story by Rousseau, Little Red Riding Hood is a teenager. At the end she gets into the bed with the wolf and he "eats her up!" The tale was written, not as a folk tale, but as a specific warning to young females of his time to beware of "wolves" without furry tails. It was written in a folktale format because that was a highly popular format at the time. Victorian versions of the story offer more characters to the story. A bird family in a nest of a tree along the way, a woodsman or hunter each of whom is aided by Little Red Riding Hood and each does some act to save and protect the girl and her grandmother from the wicked wolf.

How old is a fairytale Grandma? Within her age range, how does she dress, how does she walk. She is mostly portrayed as elderly and she wears her grey hair pulled into a bun in back, her voice cracks or wavers when she speaks and she often walks awkwardly with a cane.

She could have white hair with a purple streak, dress in more currently fashionable clothing and do workouts in the gym. Many elderly women do, these days. Also in a modern recreation all characters are affected by age and health, personality and/or the current styles of contemporary times. Breaking old fashioned clichés is important to keep puppetry up to date in the world of storytelling.

Puppet parents are adults and exact age, again, is generally unimportant to the audience.

The age still might or could affect the acting and the presentation. Age factors in plays will affect all family members, which can allow for great comedic fun when appropriate. The ages of Hansel and Gretel will affect the ages of their parents.

Ages of imaginary characters are up for grabs. How old is the wolf? Imagination may lope on forever. How old is an immortal Greek god? An ogre? A devil's demon? A witch, a warlock or a wizard?

How old is a fairy, an elf, a gnome or a troll? Do any of these ages really matter? How old are the three little pigs? Are they all the same age? Walt Disney made them all exactly alike, same age, same sex, same attitudes, same clothing maybe in different colors and they did have different names. Character ages depend on the play as interpreted from the tale, the director, the actor puppeteer's portrayal the characters, the age of the intended audience, and the story-play itself.

Names: Every character in theater has a name. The audience may not need to know the name; however the performer may or may not need the name as an important clue for stronger character portrayal. That would be an individual characteristic for any performer in puppetry. In puppet theater for children, teens, or adults, names may be familiar, oddball or complex, depending on the intent of the author and the intent of the story as it is being portrayed.

The writer's taste and judgement are the controlling factors. Never name a puppet character after someone well known by the writer or performer, and especially not a favorite son, daughter, niece or nephew. The known name may subconsciously control the shaping of the story, the acting, and emotions within the play.

Often a puppeteer has problems with finding names for characters; baby naming books and old telephone books are good resources. There are several books of names created for writers of various forms of plays and novels.

Physical, Mental, Emotional & Social Characteristics

Every character in a play is a very specific being with his or her own established personal characteristics. Every part needs to be a specific person to the actor, director and the rest of the cast in the play and eventually to the audience.

Every bit part needs at least one viable and important speech or scene within the play, otherwise leave them out of the play. In human theater the expense of hiring an actor who has no reason for being in the play makes these "bit parts" unviable. In puppet theater, the time and energy to build and costume a character who only has a walk-on bit is a great deal of hard work for nothing. One good informative speech to the character who only appears briefly will perhaps make the effort worthwhile.

In theater, even crowds have personalities and reasons for being together. The crowd fleeing from the monster is terrified, and the crowd trying to kill the monster is obviously an angry mob. The crowd cheering the heroic knight in shining armor is delighted, and every other crowd has a reason for being in a mood. Two crowds at the same time may have different attitudes but generally in conflict about the same subject, "Kill the murderous beast!" or "Save the rare and beautiful creature!"

Physical: The physicality affects how a character behaves or functions. Each character is affected by their personal physicality not by stereotypes or older versions of fairy tales. In other words, physicality is not separate from personality.

The physical qualities alone fill a list as long as the combined Nile and Amazon rivers. The list includes general appearance: tall, short, a small person, musclebound, handsome, anywhere from hideously ugly to gorgeously beautiful. The physical may go from slender, skinny as a stick, pleasingly plump to obese, distorted with minor or major bodily malfunctions or injuries, humpback, temporary or permanent injury, birth defect, ugly as sin, pleasantly attractive, beautiful as a goddess or disgustingly ugly, disfigured, visible bruises or wounds, and on into infinity. With villainous characters it is wise to avoid *too many* negative characteristics or the villain may inadvertently become comical. The physicality of any character will affect how they walk, move, think, care about themselves and other characters.

A teenage girl, on prom night, would be horrified and go into a panic to find a zit on her nose, while a comic old witch might be delighted a new zit or wart.

 In times past, human deformities were considered comical, Mr. Punch with a big nose and a hump back and Cyrano with his huge nose. A one legged man with a crutch, the little people, or one who stutterers or lisps, the fat person trying to look nice, the woman with a rolling pin as her cudgel, a crazy old wise man, odd mismatched clothing or exaggerated fashions, big noses, et cetera. These characters have been used as comical imagery for hundreds of centuries but in today's society one is expected to be more sensitive in using imperfections and injuries for comedy.

In an Irish folk tale, a young man who has a hump back and a gimpy leg is in love with a farmer's beautiful daughter. A leprechaun magically changes him into a handsome and fit young man. He goes to woo the girl only to discover she is in love with that kind and gentle young man with a hump back and a gimpy leg. The youth must recapture the leprechaun to be changed back into himself, which he eventually does and happily woos and wins the young colleen.

Mental: Every character has different mental attributes. That mentality may be anything from stupid, idiotic or silly to brilliant and worldly wise, book wise, and/or street wise, usually one only but sometimes both at once. A character might be clever but uneducated or have numerous high college degrees with brilliant knowledge and little or no practicality or common sense. Such a character could be a cliché that may embarrass or anger some, but these qualities have been used in comedy for at least a few thousand years.

Some children may be well behaved, some may be brats, or, more realistically, happy children who may have behavioral problems from time to time. Some witches are mean and scary, some humorous but wicked, and some simply silly or comical in their wickedness and sometimes beautiful on the outside and wicked in the mind. Some people are rumor spreader and gossips, others are secretive and some ungiving and unforgiving.

Who is the character? There is a great range of creative and imaginative mental possibilities, just as there is a whole range of human personalities in this wonderful but not always forgiving world. Give every character its own personality within the intent of the play as a whole. Every character must have at least one important speech or contribution to the play, or leave them out.

Emotional: Happy, sad, angry, polite, phony by being too polite, impolite, rude, calm and gentle, mean, cantankerous, sweet, kind, excessively worried, easily upset but easily calmed, strong and handsome or strong and plain, egotistical, shy, full of hate, full of life and vitality, full of envy, jealous, secure and in control, flirtatious, outrageously vulgar or given to bragging, easily angered, artificially kind, open and willing to laugh.

Emotions are often expressed in an outer and almost obvious ways, but they may also be shown quite subtly through more delicate expressions for adults or older children, but usually more obvious for young children.

Social: Puppet characters may be social or antisocial, depending on the story needs. What does each character think about the self and the other characters? How do the other characters think about the one in question? Certainly not always the same. In most theater for adults, the characters are more strongly pictured by both their personalities and their behaviors. In children's theater, characters are more simplified as personalities and enriched in their physical activities.

Again, characterization, motivation, and story needs to control everything within the play being presented. During every step from writing to performance, the art form requires careful, intentional thought. It is not *what* one does, but *why* and *how* one *does* it.

'He's Got the Whole World in His Hands' from
A Musical Variety Show.

9   Trying On a Character

Practice is critical to the art of theater. One must discover who your Nobody will become. Improvisation is important as a learning technique. It is a chance to practice and play. It is time to think deeply about the characters and how they fit into the whole of the show, and how they relate to the message being creating and communicated to the audience.

Improvisation is a powerful learning process but without thorough preparation and preplanning, the message may be lost in just a few moments of loose improvisation, or may also sing out loud and clear with practiced and imaginative portrayals of characters.

Never (repeat) Never read from a written script backstage. It is impossible to read, act, manipulate a puppet and communicate with an audience all at the same time. This chapter contains exercises to heighten the imagination, to envision, create, and sharpen one's characters while learning to create on the impulse of the moment. Most of these studies say *he*, but may easily be anyone, of any age, doing the skit for a reason or fill a need.

Episodes

This exercise uses a scene done three times, to demonstrate possible and flexible character variations for any of these skits.

The scene: Enter Puppet. He waves to the audience, to the left, the right and stage center. He claps his hands and blows a kiss or two to the audience, bows, waves and exits.

Variations: Who is the person coming on stage?

1. A Super Rock Star would dash onto the stage boldly waving and blowing kisses to the cheering teen audience. He might run to the center, arms wide and welcoming, clapping to his fans, He blows kisses as he exits bounding exuberantly off stage.

2. An Opera Diva would enter with a great deal of elegance. She enters grandly, slowly walks to center stage, where she curtsies deeply to the cheering audience and throws kisses to the audience. She then elegantly rises throwing more kisses and waving to the audience. Then one last kiss as she exits behind the curtain with rich and dignified finesse.

3. A Young Boy who has never been on stage or in front of an audience, is nervous and scared. He waves shakily. Embarrassed, he blows an awkward kiss to his family. He realizes he has forgotten what he was supposed to say. He runs off stage, maybe running to the bathroom because he is peeing in his pants.

What character is entering the stage in front of an audience? In doing any of the skits the puppeteer needs to create the character and the how and why the character is doing the specified activities. It is important (and fun) to be specific and detailed, the performer may improvise even in the first tries. Every character is a specific someone, doing something for intentional reasons. The puppet enters from somewhere and exits back to the same place or elsewhere for a reason. All the whys and wherefores want to be specific.

On with the Episodes

Select and think about the character appropriate for each skit. Who is doing what, why, how and how much does the character care about his chore or act or needs. Play, imagine, improvise, experiment, and, most important think, feel and care. Make them fun or tragic.

1. Enter Puppet. The puppet waves to the audience, to the left, the right and stage center. He claps his hands and blows a kiss or two to the audience, bows, waves and exits.

2. Puppet enters. He is looking for something. He looks here and there. He is upset when he cannot find the item. He searches repeatedly, but then he finds it. He picks up the item and happily carries it away as he exits.

3. Puppet enters and is very sad. He sits down slowly, and thinks sadly and cries. The crying grows into heavy keening. Slowly the crying subsides and he wipes his eyes, gets up, and sadly walks off.

4. The Puppet runs on stage. He stops suddenly and looks left, right, and upstage. He realizes he is going the wrong way. He thinks a moment but cannot remember which way. He finally decides which way to go. He turns, points in a direction and runs off.

5. The Puppet enters eagerly looking for something. He looks here and there. He becomes increasingly upset. He cannot find it. He looks almost hysterically for it. At last he throws up his arms, cries and walks off empty handed.

6. Puppet creeps on. He looks about to be sure no one is following him. He looks from side to side and finds he is alone. He rubs his hands. He looks around again, just to be sure, and tiptoes sneakily off with wicked intent.

7. Puppet walks on stage rapidly. He trips and falls. He tries to get up but there is pain. Struggling, he gets up and starts to cry. He rubs his painful knee. He slowly limps off in pain.

8. Puppet walks rapidly onto the stage. He looks around for a friend. He looks left and right several times. He cannot see his friend. Then he spies the friend far away. He waves and dashes off to join the friend.

9. Puppet walks on looking for someone. He sits down and waits. He looks again, taps the stage impatiently and looks around for the someone. He becomes still more impatient. He waits some more, then gets up frustrated and angrily exits.

10. Puppet enters slowly and is very tired. He yawns, stretches. Then he cleans off a spot on the stage and lies down. He goes to sleep and begins to snore. He snores louder, He snores so loudly he wakes himself up, gets up, yawns, stretches, and refreshed, walks energetically away.

On the Other Hand

Now put the Nobody on the non-writing hand and do the playlets again. Perform each skit differently. There is no one way to do any of these pieces, be creative and imaginative. Stretch your ideas and use the creative powers, learning, growing to become a performer of greater artistry, richer comedy and more dramatic power.

Groups Working Together

When groups are working together, it is important to offer some form of thoughtful *Response Session* after playing the scene. Viewers should express likes, positive opinions and suggestions for possible improvement. It is wise to understand these are *not* to be *critical reviews* but learning sessions for helping and growing in positive ways. It is wise to begin with a compliment or two, then ask questions about a bit that was unclear or make a suggestion for possible improvements.

Always finish a response with a positive statement.

Double Duty Demi-Dramas

Now, put a Nobody puppet on each hand and do the sketches below. As a broad guide line, one puppet moves and the second figure pauses. The second figure responds to the first who pauses while the second moves. This helps the audience to see and know what a puppet is doing.

When two puppets are active at the same time, the audience gets confused. They cannot watch two different things at once. When the script says the puppets are walking in together or doing something as one, they move together. Generally, in a dance, a search, and even in a fight, one figure moves, then the second figure responds. This also applies when two puppets are talking to each other, one speaks and the other listens and then the second figure answers and the first one listens.

Remember the Tortoise and the Hare. "Slow and steady wins the race."

1. One Puppet enters looks about and waits. Figure Two enters looks about and sees figure One. They hurry to each other, shake hands or hug and greet hello. First puppet

indicates the second figure should come with him. They walk out happily together.

2. Two puppets are sleeping (center stage). One wakes up and tries to wake the other. The second puppet keeps falling back to sleep repeatedly. The first puppet tries multiple times to wake the first, then he gives up, shrugs in disgust, lies down and goes back to sleep.

Note: To move the two puppets off while still in their sleeping position, lift the two characters up with a tiny tuk, the slowly lower them down behind stage together.

3. Puppet One enters happily and sits down on the playboard. The second enters and sees the happy one. Two is angry and shows it. One tries to calm the other by performing crazy stunts. Two begins to chuckle, gets happy and laughs and they go off together laughing out loud.

4. Two puppets meet. One starts to cry. The other tries to comfort the crier, finally the crying one starts to giggle and laugh. They laugh together then go off together laughing happily!

5. One puppet comes on stage slowly. The second creeps up behind him and scares him. The first puppet jumps up in surprise then faints. The second puppet tries several times to awaken the first but cannot. The second drags the fainted figure off stage.

6. One puppet runs on and trips and falls. The second puppet comes on and tries to help the first get up. They struggle in their efforts and they both fall down. They struggle to get up and each one helps the other, both limping off stage.

7. One puppet is asleep on stage and snoring peacefully. Another puppet sneaks on and tip toes around, looking for something. The first figure wakes up and tries to catch the first one. The second figure run off and the first runs off chasing after him.

8. Two puppets meet. They get into a fight. They fight for a while, then both fall down. Pause. They get up one by one, and apologize and become friends again. They go off together.

9. Two puppets are walking together. One sees something and tries to make the other look. He won't. The first keeps trying to show the second what is there. Finally they both look and run off. (The puppeteer must know *what* is seen, *why* and *where* they go, with what attitude.)

10. One puppet is trying to lift something. It is very heavy. The second figure comes on and tries to help. They cannot lift the item. They struggle, but cannot lift it. They try several times to pick it up. They cannot. They both go off.

All of these pieces may be done over differently for experience and learning. Any of these double pantomimes could be done by one puppeteer or two puppeteers. If there are two performers, the puppets are usually on the outside hands. In some cases the reverse will work better. Try it and see. Invent some of your own practice pantomimes and skits. In all of these pieces, one is not performing for one's self, one is communicating the ideas to the viewers, even if, in practice, there are no viewers. Assume they are there.

Raccoon Tales

10   Properties & Props Alive

Now that one has established and played with character and experimented with the limits and breadths of character motivations, and storytelling, it is time to explore accessories that solidify the character's identity and motivation.

For glove puppets, this is typically done through props, actions and theatrical motivations. One of the great advantages of the glove puppet is the ability to use and handle objects (actor's properties) better than most other puppet types.

Cinderella can sweep with her broom, or dance with it dreaming of the ball. Little Red Riding Hood may put goodies into her basket, Johnny Appleseed chops wood with his trusty ax and then takes a swig of cider from his jug. Ophelia may pick wild flowers before she falls into the stream. Hamlet can pick up the skull to expound on poor Yorik to Horatio, Lady Macbeth can sleep walk while carrying a candle, she can put the candle down to rub her hands, and later pick the candle up and walk away. Punch and Judy will have their battles with the slapstick and mop. The crocodile and the dog easily bite Mr. Punch's long nose, much to Judy's delight.

Puppets can play pianos, guitars, trumpets and other musical instruments, they can read, write with a pen, draw pictures, pick flowers and put them into a vase. Puppets can fight with swords, pick flowers in a field, find and read the treasure map, dig with a shovel for the pirate's treasure and almost anything the script or story may require.

Props React to Puppets

Props may also take on characteristics of their own.

In response to the character's motives or needs as part of the message the play conveys to the audience. For example, the character in Becket's *"Act Without Words #1"* can climb the tree, stack up the boxes and try to get the pitcher of ice water down and the ice water can move itself out of reach and mock the thirsty man. A hobo can rummage through a trash bin, which can react to the hobo negatively or positively. The hungry hobo may spy an apple in a tree and work feverishly to get the fruit, he then collapses with exhaustion and crawls away sadly. The apple then might slowly descend from the tree to the ground and the tree can laugh, wickedly or humorously as the performer chooses.

Pandora may open the forbidden trunk and its contents may speak or act out their own intents. Two puppets can lay a tablecloth on a table and spread out the wrinkles and the tablecloth may refuse to remain neat and wrinkle its self again. How might the puppets solve the problem?

A prop may dance around a room and do its deeds without a puppet handling it. A Victorian lass may flirt with her fan and when the Beau rejects her, the fan may fly from her hand, torment the jilting beau and chase him from the room.

There are many options to experiment with, but be careful not to overdo. Try using all the choices possible, then select what works best for you and the audience.

Properties Large and Small

Some props are larger in proportion to the puppet in order for the puppet to handle it. Larger often allows the audience to see it more clearly and an over-sized prop may often be wonderfully comedic. In other plays, very small props may be made larger than reality without appearing comical.

Sergei Obratzov, a great puppeteer of Russia, was doing a piece where a puppet was drinking too much vodka. The vodka bottle was a small puppet size bottle. On one tour, he forgot to pack the small bottle. He arrived at the performance and could find only a large human sized vodka bottle which he was forced to use instead.

The audience roared with laughter far more richly than with the smaller bottle. Not only that, but the act of over-drinking was made visually stronger with the larger bottle. He never used the small prop bottle again.

The performer must create the illusion the puppet is using the prop. If the audience can plainly see the human hand within the puppet figure is handling the prop, the illusion is lost. Observation, practice and visualization usually work very well together.

The following simple actions are learning exercises, and may be practiced with controlled study and experimentation. Most of these exercises could be made into fine pieces of puppet curtain raisers, preludes or etudes.

• Mops • Brooms • Shovels • Ladders • Et All •

Long handled items like mops, brooms or shovels are wonderful in puppet tales.

Cinderella might use a broom or mop in several ways. Certainly she would sweep the floor so her step mother would not be angry, or with agitation because she is frustrated over the burden of cleaning up after her sisters. In simple sweeping moves the puppet can easily handle the prop, so the audience sees the puppet using the prop rather than seeing the puppeteer's hand gripping the prop from within the puppet. Props can be easily modified so the appearance of sweeping is easier.

By attaching a rod at the brush end of a broom and manipulating it with the puppeteer's other hand below the audience's sight may make the sweeping seem more believable.

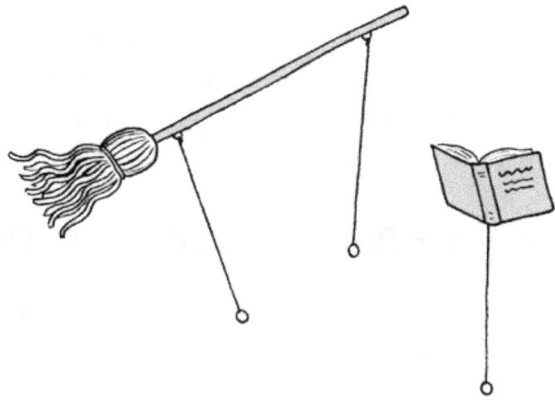

This kind of rod is also wonderful for a witch character stirring a pot of potent brew. The witch can move away to get another ingredient while the broom continues to stir the brew by itself. A witch stirring her magic brew with a large spoon holds the spoon with both hands and stirs in a circular motion. The witch's pot should be oversized for humor and so the witch can stir in a large visible way.

Likewise, a pirate is digging for the hidden treasure and the shovel gets tired of digging and refuses to do the pirate's bidding.

A shovel from a child's sand pail is about the right size for a glove puppet in these practice routines, it is way too large and just perfect! Perfect for practice, humor and discovery. For a finished piece, the shovel would be hand-made to fit in with the play's design and intent. Make certain it looks as if the puppet character is holding the shovel rather than the human hand inside the puppet.

The puppet pushes the shovel in to break the top surface of the dirt, then pushes deeper to fill the shovel blade, lifts the heavy load and then dumps it. The puppet might toss (the nonexistent) dirt over its up-stage (away from the audience) shoulder or just in front of where he is digging as a prop resembling a pile of dirt slowly rises from below. Make the action a good visual detail. At the end of the digging the puppet might insert the shovel into a pocket on the back of the fake dirt as if the shovel was stuck into the dirt, or the puppet might sling the shovel onto his shoulder and walk off stage with it. Other digging or shovel activities may be tried, experimenting with the story needs of the character. Play with the ideas to see where they go before building the show.

Nobody Learns to Read

If a character needs to read, use a book similar to a small child's book, about 4" X 6" closed. Since the puppet's eyes do not move (nor would they be seen if they did), the puppet must "trick" the audience into thinking it is reading. Have a puppet begin to read by opening the book and looking at the right hand page. Pause for a fraction of a second, then turn the head slowly from left to right across the page. Stop with a small tuk. Then turn the head quickly to the left, again with a tuk, and slowly read the next line. Does anyone remember the old fashioned manual typewriter? Same moves, different intents.

Once the puppet appears to be reading the book, the performer may try variations on the techniques for reading for more meaningful or comedic experiments rather than simply reading across the page. Try having your character read something sad, funny, or surprising. How would your character read directions for a project? How would the character read to study for a test? Is the character a slow reader or a fast reader?

Again, in puppet theater, the book may also be a living, thinking being. The character really wants to study but the book does not want to be read. How might one communicate to the audience the book has a mind of its own and is also very stubborn? How many ways can the book show the audience it does not wish to be read? How does one inform the audience the other frustrated character really wants to read?

Try the reverse. The character does not want to study and the book really wants him to. How many ways can the book communicate its needs and desires to be read without any spoken words? Might it poke the nonreader on the shoulder to insist, or simply open and jump in front of the character's face. It might snuggle up and try to get flirty and cozy. Show the glove puppet does not want to read. How might the puppet reject the insistent or flirtatious book that wants to be read?

Experimenting and playing with props to discover new possibilities is as important as rehearsing with them. Have fun, be adventurous and experimental, find new ways and stretch the imagination to the fullest extent.

A Bouncing Ball

A solid rubber ball with a thin but strong steel rod inserted and glued is a great prop to communicate with the audience. The puppeteer controls the ball with one hand, the puppet is on the other. By playing and experimenting, one can seek and discover how many moves the props may do.

When a real rubber ball is tossed into the air it goes up in an arc, slowing as it reaches the peak of the arc then continuing down it gains speed as it falls. It will hit the bottom and bounce up again fast, but not quite as high as the first time, slowing at the peak and gaining in speed as it falls, then, again, the ball rebounds at the bottom, and so on until it loses its power. The ball bounces get smaller and smaller and eventually the ball simply rolls to a stop.

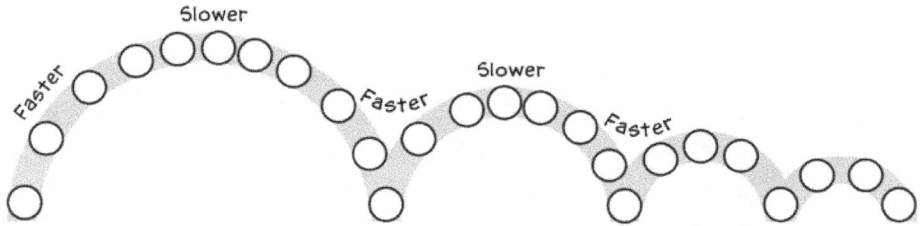

Now have the puppet character play with the ball in different ways. The ball might bounce in slow motion or faster than the eye can see. The puppeteer can, with practice, control the ball to do anything needed within a performance. How many wild and wonderful tricks can the two characters accomplish? The ball becomes a character with a personality when it appears to be in control of itself and plays or tricks the puppet. This could be a fine episode in the story of the *Frog Prince*. The Princess is playing with the ball. Give the ball a personality, too. What tricks can the ball play on the Princess before it falls into the well? How does the daughter of the King respond to the ball's tricks? How does the Frog manage the ball? Does he also have trouble with it? Are the frog and ball in cahoots to fool the Princess? Create a relationship, good or bad between a puppet and a prop, and Voila! – Puppet theater happens.

Props that Look Real

To communicate well with the audience, each prop needs to give the appearance of reality even when they are not realistic. Handmade props are usually far better for a puppet play than most store bought items. If using bought items as props, be sure they are within the overall design of the total production. Often the things that are ready-made look too commercial for a puppet prop. It is so much better when the design is adjusted or adapted to fit the puppet play.

How the prop is handled communicates its "theatrical" weight, which is important to the character and the physical act of handling a prop.

Drinking glasses are a big problem. The cheap plastic glasses from the party supply store look like cheap plastic glasses from the party store. Real glass breaks too easily if the puppet drops it. Often bridal shops have various "puppet-sized" drinking vessels of fairly strong plastic used for holding nuts or other small snacks, for a sip or two of brandy, and so on. Very antique drinking vessels that look like carved wood (hint, hint), golden goblets or drinking horns or gourds can be handmade of any number of easily available sculpting materials, and decorated to be appropriate for the story and consistent with the puppet and scenic design.

When the play calls for a puppet to lift a goblet or a candle or any other small prop, add an upside down "L" shaped handle that the puppet hand can slip into from below and appear to pick up and put down the prop. Take care the handle is big enough to accept the human fingers, or thumb, without getting too big for stability. Also note such a prop needs to be fairly lightweight to function well.

Handmade plants and flowers, or flat painted and cut out images are usually far better than commercial lifelike and life-size plastic or faux silk flowers. The realistic silk flowers will probably conflict with the design of hand-made puppet figures and make the puppets look unreal by comparison. In some places the appearance of the flower is so important to the tale that a realistic blossom may be the right choice. Again it is not what one does, but how and why one does the whatever.

Costumes as Objects of Expression

Part of a puppet's costume might also be a usable prop. A cook or servant may wipe their hands on their apron. Other costume props can be hats, scarves, shoes, gloves capes and even hairdos. In Beckett's *"Waiting for Godot"* one character has to struggle to pull his shoe off, shake the sand out of it and put the shoe back on again. In my Repertory Puppet Theater production, I made a boot just large enough to slide on and off the foot, with no laces to untie and retie. Since I was working both characters on stage, my partner performed the task of removing the boot from the foot, the character only appeared to struggle removing the boot. Shaking the sand out was easy. Putting it back on was just a little push from below although we made it seem to be comedically problematic.

In the National Theater of Puppet Arts' production of Shakespeare's *"Taming of the Shrew"*, Petruccio has a soliloquy: "What if she rail? I'll say she sings, as sweetly as a nightingale."

Petruccio (a glove puppet) sat, crossed and uncross his legs, leaned upon his knees, kicked up a foot to accent the various lines of his plotting speech. His legs were props with rods, not actual legs attached to the puppet. When he stood up as Katherine entered, the fake legs went down and away and the two character scene continued into the angrily flirtation scene.

In my Puppet Arts production of *Punch and Judy*, Judy's hair, long orange curls, were props for her to express her emotions of the moment. She fluffed them up to look more well kempt, "flung them out with her hands in anger; twiddled them in her hands when worried. Punch also pulled on them. As much a prop as part of herself.

In Lady Macbeth's Sleep Walking Scene she sings a bit of a ditty. In the first part her joy in singing, she pulls out her cloak moving almost in a happy dance, "The Thane of Fife, He had a wife" then a brief pause she drops her cape, and she says in deep sorrow, "Where is she now?"

The dropping of her cape expressed her sudden change of emotion, and expressed her madness.

In *Bingo, the Circus Dog*, the wicked magician Fargo, in planning a dastardly deed, swings his cape around and covers the lower part of his face, a classic villain move, then runs off with a theatrical flare of swirling cape. Again, the cape was used as a prop as well as a costume.

It took a great deal of repeated practice to make the cape swirl correctly every time, a light weight may have been added, but once the move was mastered it worked to great effect for the play and for the audience.

In *Rumplestiltskin* the wicked elf bowed to the King and in one rehearsal, the hat, with a long back piece and a tassel did a wonderful flip as the puppet bowed. The puppeteer had to practice the bit many times to learn to make the accidental move a permanent intended move in every performance. The small bit always got a wonderful response from audiences.

More Living Props

There are so many ways to use props in puppetry it is impossible to cover them all.

If one wants the puppets to handle or use a prop in the play, they can with imagination and practice. Sewing, hammering, cooking, writing, a bandage wrapped around an injured hand and entirely around the injured puppet head to foot, and any active business is wonderful when it is appropriate to the story and performed with observation and creativity.

The hand is the Hare, the eye is the Tortoise. The Tortoise wins the race.

Lady Macbeth's sleepwalking scene from *Macbeth*.

11   The Breath of Life

Now, as we consider how to develop a deeply artful puppet play, our attention must move from the puppet to the human performer. Just as with the puppet, the puppeteer's role and style of performance must be carefully considered to ensure the play communicates fully with the audience. This chapter and the ones following will explore the elements of what a puppeteer says and does and how they affect the success of the performance – beginning with one of the most simple and critical elements of human existence: breathing.

Puppeteers Breathe • Puppets Fake It

Breathing is essential for the maintenance of life. Breathing is one of the few bodily functions that may be controlled both consciously and unconsciously. Inhaling brings oxygen and other minor chemicals that make up the air, into our lungs which absorb the oxygen and distribute it into the bodily system. As our bodies move and function, we absorb and use the oxygen and it becomes carbon dioxide. Exhaling eliminates the carbon dioxide, other minor chemicals and a significant amount of moisture from our bodies. Athletes, performers and any physically or mentally active people need to drink more water to maintain their physical health.

Most people breathe unconsciously without thinking about breathing, and often that is all that is necessary.

A simplistic explanation is, when at rest, the body needs less oxygen so the breathing is fairly shallow. When active, the carbon dioxide in the blood increases due to the activity, which starts both increased heart beat and the internal respiratory center. This causes the diaphragm to pull down, making more room for the lungs to expand, thus increasing the intake of oxygen on the inhale then releasing the excess carbon dioxide, other chemicals and moisture on the exhale. After a hearty workout, running or any physical or mental pressure, we breathe more heavily causing the storing of far too much carbon dioxide in the system. The panting and heavier breathing is ridding the body of the unwanted gases and taking in the much needed oxygen.

The emotional and physical demands made upon a performer requires a strong knowledge and control of the process of breath and breathing. Actors, singers, dancers, acrobats, athletes and speechmakers must all learn to control their breathing to fulfill their physical prowess. Joggers, physical laborers and many others need to use the conscious practice of breath control. Unfortunately most people, as they grow toward adulthood, do not learn to breathe properly for good health.

The illustration of the vocal mechanism on the next page shows there are two major passages from the nasal cavity and vocal palate down into the body. The *trachea*, the frontal tube takes air in and out of the lungs with every breath taken.

The rear "pipe" is the *esophagus* which carries just chewed food down to the stomach to be digested for the body's nourishment. At the upper joining of the *trachea* and the *esophagus*, is the *epiglottis*, a fleshy lid or cap, that opens on the *esophagus* when swallowing and closes on the *trachea*. The *epiglottis* opens the *trachea* when we breathe or speak and closes on the *esophagus*, thus controlling the proper functions of each.

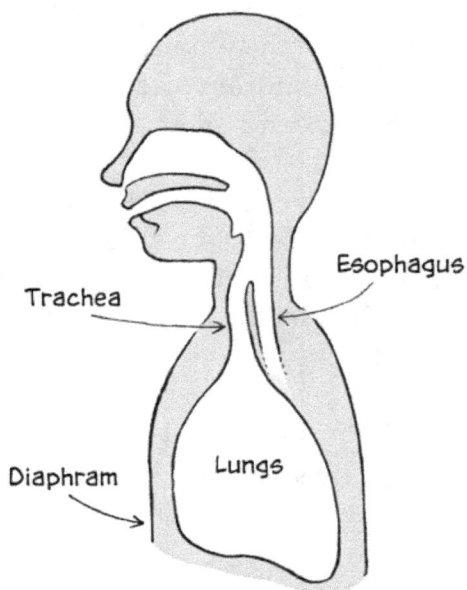

It is often said one should not talk with one's mouth full. It looks unpleasant to fellow diners. The truth is, if a person eats and talks at the same time, the *epiglottis* may malfunction and the food may very well go into the *trachea* rather than the *esophagus*. This makes breathing anywhere from difficult to impossible. That is how and why the Heimlich maneuver was discovered. It is also why one should always listen to one's mother, "Don't talk with your mouth full!"

Many teachers of breath and breathing state chest breathing is incorrect and diaphragmatic breathing is the only proper way to breathe. Both of the aspects of breath are healthy and very usable breathing practices in daily life and in professional performances. In theater, it is not so much a question of breathing "correctly" as understanding and putting into practice the proper uses of the lungs and *diaphragm* for both vocal projection and personal voice protection.

Using the differences between shallow and deep breathing is a tool for health but it also allows puppeteers to perform for theatrical needs in expressing a character, a scene or important emotional activities within the whole of a production. It is also essential for projecting the natural voice in a large auditorium without the need of microphones and other accompanying sound equipment.

Stand tall and erect, in good posture, but relaxed, arms hanging down comfortably to the sides. Breathe in through the nose a shallow breath of air. Feel the lungs and ribs expand as the lungs take in the air, then let the air out through the mouth in a non-vocalized "sss" position.

The shoulders should not move up and down when practicing breathing. The shoulders have nothing to do with good breathing practices, speech or vocalizing.

Feel the lungs and the ribcage expand and contract with each breath. This expansion is a natural function and takes the breath in quickly.

A gasp, which is simply a sudden intake of air, may be performed both physically and emotionally to express less dramatic moments, a gentle appreciation a surprise of pleasure, disappointment or anger, a gasp of truth or positive or negative surprise. Even the last rasping breath of life is often a form of gasp.

Deeper diaphragmatic breathing is needed in larger auditoriums and performance venues. The volume during highly dramatic scenes also demands more breath than quiet scenes.

Heavier emotional activities of anger or fear require the full breath from the diaphragm. Breathing from the diaphragm, take in a large breath of air through the nose. Hold the breath and let the air out through the mouth with a non-vocalized "sss" breath.

Feel the diaphragm expanding and contracting as you breathe. On becoming aware of the breath and breathing possibilities, with a frequent amount of practice, the breath will come naturally and be there automatically when needed in performing. Even the complexity of rehearsing new material requires more breath and energy as do the public performances. And drinking extra water is important.

The puppeteer and teacher, Nikki Tilroe, had her classes sit cross legged on the floor with the arms loosely hanging. A hand is gently placed on each hip to form the imagined picture of a deflated tire. The class then slowly filled that tire with air, breathing in with one long slow breath through the nose, their arms slowly expanding out to suggest the inflating of a tire.

When fully inflated the class sits for a moment, holding the breath in, with the arms out as the fully inflated tire, noting how the body feels filled with the air in the fully expanded lungs and diaphragm.

Now the students imagined the just-filled tire has a very tiny leak and very slowly lets the air leak out with a "sss" hissing sound, and the arms slowly pull in towards the body as if the tire was deflating until there was no more air to leak out and the tire had gone flat. One long and very slow breath in, held in and then one long slow breath out, feeling the expansion of the lungs and diaphragm on the inhale, slow collapsing of the breathing mechanism on the deflation. The vocalized hiss or "sss" sounds are caused by the force of the air pushing out of the mouth without using the vocal folds.

Another exercise for increasing and controlling the breath is to find a book, preferably an old and boring text book with long dull paragraphs. Take a long deep breath and hold it. Begin reading aloud without breathing between word, sentences or paragraphs. When the breath runs out, mark the place in the book with a small arrow sticky-tab. Do not use a pencil or pen to mark because the good old boring book may be ruined.

The next day do the same thing beginning at the starting point and trying to hold the breath longer than before and read farther into the book. Again, mark the spot with the same tab when the breath runs out. Repeat this exercise every day for a full week. Most people read far longer each day as the exercise is repeated day after day.

Normal breathing habits, and breathing for performance, all need to be practiced on a regular schedule. Acting on stage and performing multiple characters in a play will require good breathing techniques to accomplish an artful play that communicates with the audience. Once the controlled breath and breathing becomes a habit, it will last a lifetime. Of course, working on breath and breathing, thinking about the actions of the body and breath never stops.

It is wise to do soft and heavy breathing in warming up the body before a performance or any activities requiring breathing for vocalizing or heavy physical activities. Make it a habit and a regular practice to breathe in through the nose and out through the mouth. Take a shallow breath, feel the ribs expand to make room for the enlarging lungs as they take in a shallow breath of air, and then return to the normal place as the air is exhaled out and one feels the ribs return to their natural positions.

This thoughtful, practiced breath is the foundation for the puppeteer's performance. Without it, no matter how simple it may seem, the message of the performance cannot reach the audience.

12   Speaking in Voices

In puppet theater, it's not the voice of the puppeteer that communicates with the audience, it is the voice the puppeteer gives to the puppet characters. Such voices must be crafted and practiced with care so the intent of the show comes across fully to the audience.

Puppet Characters Speak Out!

The nineteen thirties and forties were often called The Golden Age of Animation. Vocalist Mel Blank created voices for hundreds of the great cartoon characters and was known as *The Man of a Thousand Voices*. He created voices and personal characteristics for Bugs Bunny, Porky Pig, Woody Woodpecker, Daffy Duck, Tweetie Pie and Sylvester the Cat, Wile E. Coyote, Speedy Gonzales, Barney Rubbles and a many others from the *Loonie Toons* and *Merrie Melodies* cartoon series.

Frank Oz, also created many voices for characters in *The Muppets* television programs and on *Sesame Street*. He strongly stated he did not do *puppet* voices, he created *character* voices. The point, of course, is to work at creating good and interesting theatrical characters rather than foolish, silly, trite or simply amusing voices. Some humorous vocal sounds, qualities and comic characters can prove highly entertaining to the audience. However, use good sense and good judgement. High and very squeaky voices may harm the speaker's voice and will often hurt young children's ears, while very deep and out of depth voices may be garbled and unintelligible to audiences and stress may cause serious damage to the vocal mechanism.

You are creating theatrical plays with both serious and comedic characters and/or situations. The voices must be strong and honest and may be highly comedic or soulful for the right characters, in the right situations, not necessarily realistic, but with rich character portrayal.

The Vocal Mechanism at Work

In your own voice, say a simple line without acting.

Listen to the natural quality of the voice. You might recite a simple line such as, "Hello, Mr. Smith. I am glad to see you up and about." It is not important what one says in this learning process, but how and why one is saying it. Do not try to think up a new line or speech each time, wasting time thinking of clever things to say. It is far more important to listen to the quality of the vocal sounds as the lines are spoken. *Never* use a line from a play in progress or in an upcoming or future play.

Repeating the same line several times and listening closely to the sound of your own voice will help: listen and sense the vocal quality of the sounds and the meanings behind the words as they are spoken. When speaking in casual conversations, you may hear your own voice, but you seldom really listens to it. A speaker is thinking about what they are saying. The performer must also listen to *how* they are saying it and try the line with several meanings and emotions behind the line.

By recording your voice and listening to the play back, you can learn a great deal about your own voice and good or bad personal speech habits. Listen carefully to your voice. Peojple are often shocked when hearing their own natural speaking voice on a recording. That is partly because most people do not really listen to how they sound because they are thinking about the thoughts being expressed. Also since the voice is issuing from many areas within the human body, it vibrates vibrate differently in the speaker's ears than when it is recorded electronically.

Raise the voice in pitch by several musical notes on the scale: "do, ray, mi fa, sol" and repeat "Hello, Mr. Smith, I am so glad to see you up and about." It sounds different from the usual speaking voice because the effort of raising the voice up several notes changes the sound quality.

With the natural voice going down in pitch from the usual range of the speaker's voice, the same "do, ti, la, sol, fah" scale notes below the normal range, and repeating the line. "Hello, Mr. Smith I am very glad to see you up and about."

Again, the effort of lowering the voice makes a vocal sound quite different from the natural speaking voice. Listen carefully to the lowered voice and play with the sound.

Practicing these various pitch levels in high, medium and low will give the speaker a beginning and better understanding of their own voice. Going higher without hurting the voice and lower to a comfortable tone, you can easily comprehend the beginnings of the vocal capacity and the beginnings of character voice creation.

Avoid created voices that strain the natural voice to accomplish them. Low gravely voices can be very harmful to some voices and just fine with others. When those low and gravely voices are maintained within the natural vocal palate, rather than forcing the voice into the actual vocal fold, one may find a good and stable deep or gruff voice without strain. Each puppeteer actor must find their own voices, their own capabilities and their own problematic speech habits.

Many men with deep baritone or bass voices, and women with alto or contralto voices, may be able to go up into a lovely smooth falsetto, which in professional singing is referred to as *head tones* and when the voice is down to the lower level of their natural voice the sound are referred to as *chest tones*.

These voice changes will help you to create a much greater range of voices. Others will discover the various techniques, voices and tones that will work best for them. Not everyone, but most people, can change their voices enough to create different and usable character voices, and that is what these practices bring out. How wide a range of voices may be created without hurting or straining the voice? That would be very personal and individual. Some voices will be more flexible and others, less. It is important to find the flexibilities in your own natural voice.

Work to make them the most flexible within your range of vocal sound. Then, in creating the puppet characters for a script, most puppeteers can usually do it with great skill and wit and without strain. Keep the voice safe and use the inner vocal palate and not the actual center of the chords at the Adam's apple.

Placement of the Voice

The voice may be placed in the front, middle or back of the vocal palate. Each person habitually has the voice placed in one of those parts of the palate which is part of the naturalness of one's own speech practice. Different people place their voices in different points in the vocal palate which affects the quality of the tone and vocal quality in which one usually speaks.

No one place is better than the other, and everyone will find the location of their own voice as a matter of *habit*, rather than nature's placement by force. Repeating the "Hello, Mr. Smith" line in your own natural voice, listen to the placement of the voice.

Listen closely to find and feel where your voice is usually comfortable and generally used position. Again, the voice may be in the front of the mouth just behind the teeth, or in the center of the mouth responding through the vocal palate, or in the softer palate in the back of the mouth.

If the voice is set just behind the teeth it needs to be pushed out, consequently the voice has a sharp edgy quality to it. If the voice is placed in the center of the palate the voice is less sharp, but still strong and natural, if set to the back of the palate the voice becomes softer and a bit less powerful and one has to use more intentional thrust to speak louder.

Also note the vocal qualities change in each of the positions. Listen and practice and interpret what variables happen in each of the individual placements.

Pitch

Speak a line in one's normal tone. Now raise the voice up a few notes, "do, ray, mi, fa, sol" notes, repeat the practice line again and listen to the voice. In this higher range there is a change in the vocal quality simply by changing the pitch of the voice. Note the vocal sounds.

Lower the voice a few notes down "do, ti, la, sol, fah and repeat the line, "Hello, Mr. Smith", the sounds may be richer and stronger. Each person's voice will create the tone differently. Push the voice forward the sound quality changes. Centralize the voice at this lower level and the act of lowering the voice changes the sound quality.

Taking the voice up a few notes higher, "do, ray, mi, fah, sol" Listen to the difference when pushed hard through the teeth, set in the middle palate and pushed to the softer back of the vocal palate. All of these qualities are the beginnings of interesting and usable character voices.

Discover the varieties of sounds in one's own natural voice.

Now experiment to find still more qualities to make the voice give sound to many different kinds of personalities. Having worked on placement and pitch, move into tone, color and texture.

Tone, Color and Texture: Musical,

• Flat • Nasal • Harsh • Velvety • Raspy • Clear •

Using the normal speaking voice, the puppet actor recites the "Mr. Smith" line, adding just a bit for ease of hearing the changes in a very musical, almost but not quite a singing style.

"Hello, Mr. Smith. I am so glad to see you up and about."

Mr. Smith answers, "Thank you, and now I am feeling much better these days."

Now make the first part of the line in a higher musical voice and the answer in the lower voice. *Voila!* It begins to sound like a conversation between two different characters.

Try the same things in different character voices, one high and one low pitched. Listen to the voices very carefully as the lines are spoken. Where is the natural voice in comparison with these slightly distorted voices? Saying the line in each of the vocal placements and through the nasal passages. What kinds of characters do these variations in register suggest?

Try the "Mr. Smith" lines again in a smooth velvety voice and a nasal voice, or a harsh voice (being certain that the harshness is in the palate, not the larynx).

Playing with Speech:

• Diction • Gu-Du-Du • Pronunciation • Pitch • Texture • Slang •

Now go through the various voices with characteristic speech habits. Experiment with other vocal peculiarities. One must, at this stage, constantly listen to the sounds being made, for example: tom<u>A</u>toes or tom<u>AH</u>toes, hea<u>R</u>t or ha<u>AH</u>t. Using the language of "Gu-du-du" such as "I godda gu tu du doctuh." or "Didja eat jet?" "Nah, diju?" "Nah, Squeat!"

Repeat these voices, making sure the audience will grasp *what* is being said as well as how it is being said. If one overdoes the "Gu du du" the audience may not understand and often will not listen.

One play of my own, had a line: "Come here and let me look at you." The audience giggled. I did not want a laugh in this moment. The next scene needed to get a highly comedic reaction, and this was too soon. My second performance also got a laugh on the same line. I did not like it, want it, and I did not know why I was getting an unwanted response. At the third performance on that line, a tiny voice spoke out with "bless you."

At last I knew exactly what was wrong.

The line was, "Come here and let me look at you." The character delivery sounded like, "Comeer an lemmeloo katchoo." To the young audience "Comeer an leemmeloo'" has no meaning, but "katchoo" is a very familiar sound and meaning. That unwanted laugh or giggle never happened again! Learn to listen. Listen to the audience and to the sound of the lines spoken by the characters. Listen to one's self in practice and in the realm of performance. The manner in which one says a line in theater is as important as why one says it.

Trying to make voices for someone very eloquent, very bright or very snotty depends on how the speaker interprets the lines. How might one make a "catty" woman talk? A country farmer? An old person? A child?

A Helpful Technique

Typically when Americans speak we go down on the last word of a sentence.

When performing a character with a high voice, there is a tendency to go down at the end of a sentence and continue to the next sentence a bit lower, then by going down at the end of the next sentence, and in a few lines, one has lost the higher voice. The solution to the problem will require a bit of practice to make it sound natural, but with practice and care, it will function. Once it becomes habit, it will be much to the advantage of a performer.

When you say a line in a higher voice, go up a little in pitch on the syllable or word before the last one, or even on the last word. "Hello Mr. Smith. I am glad to see you <u>up and</u> about." The "up and" is higher in tone and the "about" is at the general level of the speech. The same technique works to keep the voice low. "Howdy pal, my name is Mac <u>Spen</u>ser." Going up on "Spen" and down on "ser" will keep the voice at the correct level.

Texture:

• Delicate • Velvety • Harsh • Clear • Melodic • Raspy • Harsh •

This list is just a few of the many textural and fluid sound vibrations. Experiment with them, have fun with them, perhaps carrying the quality to extremes without hurting the voice. It is important for the puppeteer, male or female, to think about characterization rather than the simple and obvious qualities of vocal sound coloration. Many beginners often have trouble creating voices for the opposite sex characters. With practice, work and vocal exercises and a listening carefully to the opposite sex speaking, taking in color, depth and personal characteristics will help.

Speaking in a delicate voice of innocence, true or pretended, requires character study. As do all voices of complex characters. Again, it is not simply what the voice sounds like, but understanding and controlling the emotional qualities behind and within the vocal sounds.

There are so many variations in these simple qualities that it would be a true challenge to the student to create them all in these brief study pages, but when practiced over time there is no limit to possible accomplishments.

A nasal twang in a young boy's voice might make him sound impish, or it might make him sound foolish or other positive or negative qualities. Listen and practice, practice, practice. A twang in an adult voice may sound like a speech impediment, while a nasal twang as a character quality in an adult might suggest villainy. These, of course, are *clichés* which in early study will happen often. When working on a serious performance, these *clichés* must be avoided but may work well for comic situations. Remember, the choices you make as an artist affect if and how your desired message reaches your audiences.

It is not *what* one does that makes great theater, it is *how* and *why* one does it.

The Leprechan of Donegal

13 Characters Acting Up

When creating characters within a play, take them very seriously before attaching them permanently to the visual puppet figure representing the character. Voices in a puppet play are not just voices, but representations of specific characters within specific and individual behaviors and motivations. A cute squeaky voice may be fun, but is it right for the character the puppet represents? Is the character suitable for the content of the play? Before the Nobody puppet becomes the actual performance figure, the puppeteer must develop the voice of the character just as much as the character's look and mannerisms.

All puppet plays, comedic, romantic, adventurous, tragic or whatever mode the major content is, one must strive for the best possible quality within its composition and the many varying parts. Puppet character voices include speech habits, personality traits, and everything from wealth to poverty, educated to uneducated, national or foreign accents, regional dialects, and all the multiple variations within the spoken words by the individual personalities.

The following are suggestions and practice pieces for puppet character voices and speech.

Speech Habits:

• Pronunciation • Diction • Vowels • More Gu-Du-Duh •

Speech habits and vocal peculiarities are also a part of creating character voices.

Like local or foreign accents, diction, shaping of vowels (tomato or tomahto, ex<u>quis</u>ite or <u>ex</u>quisite, emu (emyu or emoo) running the words together, "itsa nelephant" or "don' as kim."

One of my favorites was a bit by a politician in conference with a reporter who asked s question and the politician answered, "Well, that's a whole nother story."

What part of speech is "nother"?

Listen to other people speaking, listen carefully as you talk with them. Listen and, especially, learn. Without making judgements, study and use the words and sound qualities for characterization.

Keep in mind the *Gu-du-du* must be made clear enough for the audience to understand, particularly for young audiences. Youngsters do not listen carefully, but they do hear what is said. The performer must speak in ways the audience will hear, understand and perceive what the dialogue is about. These needs may be met by vocal consideration, language variants, and the choice of words used to communicate.

Understanding a character, why and how they speak in the way they do, is an important learning process and should not be taken casually. Look, listen, learn and comprehend. Do not mimic, but take in to also understand the human behind the speech.

In planning plays for audiences over the age of five, one must avoid being *cute* and/or *silly* without meaning or thought behind it. Characters in plays are *symbols* of humanity with lives and emotions and inner feelings that must be portrayed to the audiences in the areas of the understanding of that audience. Also note youngsters detest "baby talk" or sounds that seem to mock children.

Pay attention, listen and learn from what is heard from the self and others.

Personality Traits:

- Phony • Shy • Confident • Insecure • Egotistical • Pretensive • Well Spoken • Happy • Laid Back • Careless • Et Cetera •

Characters with personality traits like shy, gruff, confident, insecure, stern, sweeter than honey, harsh, uncaring, leads into the next chapter on *acting*. The actor performer must care, think, practice, discover and be creative in learning to express these various ideas within the character. Some of this is obviously simple trickery, most of it is, hopefully, artist-actors trying to become the best they are capable of being.

The performer moves, observes and speaks for a character as it is being recreated anew at every performance. Speak and listen to the words being spoken. Be a critic of ones own performance and while one is performing for the audience, listen and learn, creating characters outside of reality and communicating with the audience, listening to the audience's response to the performance, thereby enhancing and perfecting the quality of the communication. There are times in performance when one out shines oneself. There are times when one goes a bit flat. Listen to the self. Listen to the character and the speech quality, listen and learn. All of this is something like being aware of the whole world as one performs.

Accents:

• Irish • Spanish • German • International • Local Accents •

The list goes on from intercontinentally to down home local. The secret to doing accents on stage is to become very familiar with the accent. One must *never* "fudge" or "fake" an accent, but become accustomed to the variants within it. Research the accent. Work on it!

Listen and talk to people with local or foreign accents to find details of the sounds and pronunciation. Practice with and talk to people who have the accent needed within the play. Find out how they feel about your interpretations of their accent. The performer works on the accent until it becomes comfortable and familiar. In performance, never *play* the accent, play the character's *emotional* needs and responses, and *allow* the accent to be a part of the vocal characterization. Also note some people feel insulted when their own national accent is improperly used.

Be careful not to use accents in false, negative, insulting or mocking ways. A stutter, lisp, or very nasal voices may also be insulting or hurtful if used improperly or for the wrong reasons.

Never make fun of an accent or speech problem, make use of them when appropriate, but with honesty and appreciation. Creating a highly comic character who has an accent is one thing, spoofing the accent itself has quite another meaning and is usually badly received. Do not make anger, make good characters and good theater.

Vocal Choreography

Picking Up Cues

Vocal arguments between two characters must also be choreographed vocally as well as physically. Two puppets arguing, controlled by one puppeteer, create problems with breathing. Actors are very strict about picking up cues. They are taught to "step" on the last word of the other actor's speech. Teachers of acting and directors often yell: "Pick up the cues! Pick up the cues!" In any puppet scene with more than one figure, the talking must flow from one character to the other - especially in puppetry by a solo performer doing an argument, or even a conversation between two puppets, one on each hand, in two different character voices. Again, the speaking must go from one character to another, picking up the cues in two different voices. Where does one breathe in a dialogue between two characters or in a vital or angry argument?

1. Never take a breath at the end of a sentence.
2. Find moments for a dramatic pause *within* a sentence to breathe.

At the beginning of the scene the puppeteer may take a very deep breath and do part of the discourse without a breath. In rapid discussion of anger or joy, speak the last word of one character and instantly go into the speech of the second speaker, find a place to take a quick breath and go on with the rapid dialogue between the two. The breathing *must not* dampen or soften the intensity of an argument or conversation.

An argument between characters is important for the audience to feel and comprehend. The discourse between two characters by one puppeteer is very difficult to do well. Practice with intent is a very good process. The puppeteer must *never* run out of breath and pant to catch the breath in the middle of any scene.

Breath and breathing are vibrant and important parts of speech in puppetry. Practice and learn to pick up cues instantly in any back and forth dialogue between two characters.

Opera sopranos, when singing major flourishes within an aria, from high to low, hitting many different vocal sounds, flourishes and tones, they must also breathe. Where they breathe will affect the fluidity and color of the music and their personal interpretation of the music. They mark on their scores where they may breathe and keep the flourish flowing within the aria.

The puppeteer playing two characters also has to breathe somewhere, and in, for example, an argument between two different characters played by the same performer, the cues within the argument must be picked up at once.

1. Never take a breath at the end of one character's speech before going on to the next character's retort. The retort must come instantly between the characters for emotional power.

2. Find places within the lines where one might take a quick breath or find a moment for a strong dramatic pause within an angry retort.

In scenes like the one below, between the Bear and the Raccoon, the speech must move rapidly between the two. During the first speech by Raccoon, the actor may breathe anywhere that is appropriate but when the Bear enters, the breathing places need to be carefully worked out. The dialogue in most of the speech would be rapid fire between the Bear and the Raccoon. Where might one breathe in dramatic pauses or thought processes without spoiling the argumentative qualities between the two characters?

(Enter RACCOON with three fish, he goes through a bit of sorting the fish in a row.)

RACCOON: Ah, that's perfect! I have caught three fish. A small fish for baby raccoon *(picks it up to show the audience and places it on the playboard)*, a medium sized fish for wife raccoon, *(Raccoon places the fish after the little one)* and a great big fish for Me! *(Which he proudly puts in place.)*

Enter BEAR:

BEAR: Ah ha! You caught some fish, and I am hungry. *(he rubs his hands)* Give me one of your fish!

RACCOON: But Bear Chief, these fish are for my family, they're hungry, too!

BEAR: I don't care about your family. I care about Me! Now give me one of your fish! Or I will eat you up, too!

RACCOON: But Bear Chief!

BEAR: Give me that fish!

RACCOON: Oh, all right, here is a fish for you! *(Hands him the very small fish)*

BEAR: Mm good! I am going to eat it up right now!

RACCOON: But Bear Chief, that fish is much too small for you.

BEAR: Small? Hey, You're right! This fish is too small! Give me a bigger fish!

RACCOON: Very well, here is a bigger fish!

BEAR: Good! I'm going to eat him up right now!

RACCOON: But Bear Chief, you don't want to eat this fish!

BEAR: Why not? I want that fish!

RACCOON: But it is sick!

BEAR: Sick! He doesn't look sick to me. Give me that fish!

RACCOON: But this fish has scales all over it!

BEAR: Scales! I don't care about scales!

RACCOON: But if you eat this fish you'll loose your fur and get scales all over you, too!

BEAR: Scales! On me? Then I don't want that fish, give me another fish!

RACCOON: All right, then, here's a bigger fish!

BEAR: Good! Gimme that fish!

RACCOON: But Bear Chief, this fish, this beautiful fish, is a mother.

BEAR: A mother!

RACCOON: A mother! And if you eat her all those little baby fish in the lake will die.

BEAR: Die?

RACCOON: Die!

BEAR: I don't care! I want that fish! Gimme that fish!

RACCOON: Wait! Why don't you catch your own fish?

These lines must go in a pace for an argument between the two with dramatic pauses or thoughts for breath and breathing. If properly acted out the breathing should happen easily, but it is a good idea to rehearse such scenes, finding the proper places for taking a quick or larger breath for the drama! This is also important so the scene is basically the same in each performance.

Puppeteers Getting into the Act

In today's puppet theater, the puppeteer is often more than just the manipulator of the figures, but also plays one or more characters in costume within the play. When this is the case, the puppeteer must consider their own role and characterization just as much as they consider that of the puppet.

Often, the puppets are manipulated in front of the audience as well as from within the puppet stage booth or on the stage scenery. This blend of puppets and live actors on stage at once may be comic, tragic, or highly imaginative with other rich ideas of humor or more dramatic works. Many plays by major playwrights could be done with a combination of puppets and people. Scenes from Shakespeare, Samuel Becket, G. B. Shaw and other highly respected playwrights have works adaptable for this combined puppet and people format. Many modern puppeteers also compose and write their plays with human actors playing characters in the puppet play of choice.

In my own production of *Aladdin*, I as puppeteer, was dressed in an Arabian inspired costume. My role was as storyteller, a popular profession in Arab nations, and the stage was decorated in theatrical designs approximating Arabic decor.

While I spoke and told parts of the tale and manipulated the puppets backstage and in front of the puppet booth. I also went backstage to manipulate scenes without being seen. The play was performed at a local museum. The music was composed and performed by a local music group directed by John Levindowsky, the show was endowed by a major arts awardIn *Beauty and the Beast*,

Paul Vincent Davis as the Storyteller and Aladdin from *Aladdin and His Wonderful Lamp*

I played the role of Beauty's father. Someone once asked me why I did not use my own voice to play the role. I responded, "I am not Beauty's father. I am an actor-puppeteer playing the role of Beauty's father. I spoke as the puppet character might speak, not as myself." Again, this is a point to be taken with some seriousness. As an artist, I must think deeply about each element of the performance. I was also playing Beauty, her two sisters, the Beast and the villainous sorcerer who turned the Prince into the Beast. My own personal ways and characteristics would be out of place in the age of the Italian Renaissance. If one is playing a character in the play, that character must be an intrinsic part *within* the play rather than something outside of it. The puppeteer/actor's role must be part of the message the play is communicating to the audience.

14   Which Comes First – The Idea or the Puppet?

Every puppet play, from beginning to end, is one variable but inviolable whole. Ideally, it is a perfect event in which every part affects, moves, changes and influences its many parts, creating a cohesive, dynamic whole. Each part must be integral to the whole, with nothing that interrupts or is out of place within that whole. That's why the puppeteer must approach every element with the utmost thought and care – from crafting the puppet character, to mastering voice and stage presence. Crafting the play itself, from idea to a fully developed show, is no different. In this part of the book we explore every step of the playwriting process, beginning in this chapter with the initial idea, so the puppet play's message reaches the audience in a compelling way.

One Play, One Plot, One Design Image, One Nest Egg Hatchling

Design of the show is a major part of puppet theater. Having the right puppets is not enough; the whole of the play must be one total world, from first opening curtain to final curtain. The play is one thing and the visual design of the puppets, props, scenery, colors and movement must all work together to cause the play to shine within its own one world.

The writing and design for a light comedy are very different from the puppets in a satiric comedy and from those created for an adventure tale, and elegant fairy tale or any other theater format. So must the scenery, props, costumes and style of the movement fit the play, making it into one world of the puppet play.

A play about very poor shepherds, whether comedy, drama or tragedy, would be very different in design, color, picture image and intent than for a play about a Prince and Princess, whether comedy, drama, romance or tragedy. This of course is obvious. The setting of the scenes, the costumes, properties and visual image of these two plays would be a world apart. A modern play set in current times would be designed very differently than a play set in the imagined future or a very ancient world, real or invented.

The tale of an adventure would need angles, strong colors and textures, while a love story would have softer and more subtle colors and more delicate images for the look to be softer. Dramatic scenes within a softer play might need to be designed slightly more dynamic than romantic, sad or tragic moments within the play.

The design of everything within the play must be specific for that play alone. Many puppeteers have one design style which they use for everything they create. This is a personal choice, but it is not the making of the finest possible puppet theater. The best, most artful puppet theater must invest all the puppeteer's creative ability into each element of each unique show, crafting each part with thought and intention

A good puppet play begins with the lights dimming up, the curtain opens, and some first image, color, scenic piece or event grabs the audience and pulls the viewers mentally and emotionally up onto the stage and into the performance. All the parts of the play must both interact and compete with all the others, but still be controlled within the whole of the play.

Lighting and color changes, background music or sounds, brightness or darkness of a scene create and change the mood throughout the show. The scenery might be simple screens of colors and patterns reflecting or suggesting the mood of the scene. A fabric with a pattern of green leaves for the scene in the woods, a red and gold brocade for the palace interior, an interesting peasant pattern for the interior of a cabin, and on and on throughout the imagination.

Some plays may need well painted pictorial scenery, another might need extremely distorted images, another might cry out for simplicity or angular shapes and forms. There is no one way except what is right for the one play being built.

The puppets are, of course, the major part of that whole and certainly not separate from it. The scenery, colors, textures and look of the puppets must all belong together as one. Highly stylized puppet figures are out of place in realistic scenery and *vice verse*.

A performance needs to bring the audience to the point of total emotional or mental emersion into the whole of all the play's many parts, from the first lights turning up to the final curtain call by the puppeteer performers.

The Egg Begins to Hatch

The egg of fine puppet theater hatches in the warm nest of the creator's imagination, mind, spirit where the many dreams and hopes are woven like the myriad sticks, twigs, leaves, mud and feathers of any bird's nest. The hatchling play slowly creates and reveals the story, the characters and the events. It taps at the inner shell of the creator's brain until the shell cracks and the first living and vivid idea is born. A new play has just begun to hatch.

In less whimsical terms, the play must come from the playwright's imagination. All the wants, needs and dreams, and the world of puppet theater begin with the strong idea, the play, the story. The momentary idea sets the mood, style and intent for the entire production. Often at some point within the creation of the play's parts, some idea may change the original format, which is fine and wonderful, so long as the finished piece is only *itself*. The tale on which the play is created may be changed in many different ways to suit the needs or ideas of the creator(s) of the play. Folk lore is inspired by tales told around the fire in the slow and cold months of winter. Grandmother's vision of the tale will be very different from Uncle Charlie's version, which would be drastically different from a small child's version. What is the playwright's version? To whom in the family group does the playwright listen?

No matter the type of story or the playwright's perspective, every play must modulate in mood and tone to create a textured show. In a high comedy, the play cannot and must not be comical throughout. One is not creating a series of comic routines, one is creating a play. At some point within the story it is important to have at least one or more sad, angry or distressing scenes of some sort to off set and underscore the comedy. In a high comedy, the audience is breathing out with heavy laughter. The several scenes of sorrow, sadness or worry, give the audience opportune moments to take in a needed, deeper, inhaled breath or two. It is also a form of contrast within the story and between the characters, the audience and the whole of the piece to keep it varied and interesting. The same is true of tragedies, and sorrowful plays. The audience is often gasping in heavy breaths with fright, fear or sorrow. Comic scenes with a tragedy allow the audiences to breathe out in laughter as a relief from the sorrowful gasping.

The Classic Play Format

The structure of a play, as observed by Aristotle in 400 BC, is still used by many contemporary play creators, and it still works. Whether you are writing for adult or child audiences, whether for live actors or handcrafted puppet characters, the basic structure is still the same.

The format is a linear timeline plot that generally runs in a straight line from the beginning to the end. The format calls for a beginning, a middle, an end, and a very brief conclusion which suggests or hints about what the future may bring.

Full length plays typically have two or three acts. In shorter puppet plays there is often only one act, but there could, might be, and often are more. Shakespeare has seven in a much longer playing time. In puppet theater a play may have more than one to three acts or a medley of short playlets to make a full length production.

A writer must know and understand the ancient format, discussed in the following section, then may use it, alter it, or break away from it with their own inventive and artistic creativity.

The BEGINNING usually introduces the protagonist (the hero) and/or other characters within the play and may or may not introduce the antagonist (the villain).

The beginning establishes the existing way of life, an equilibrium (the *status quo*), the way things are. At some point in this beginning, some interruption or change in the established order of things occurs, often caused or manipulated by the antagonist, but not, by any means, necessarily. This change from the normality within the story must occur and affect the characters and situations throughout the remaining time of the play.

The MIDDLE furthers the development of the story and may introduce one or more new characters and communicate more about these characters and the change or new situation that has happily, sadly, confusingly or tragically occurred.

This middle section also brings the characters into some sort of confrontation or conflict and usually brings the main character(s) to the point of recognition of the cause of the changes occurring in their lives.

This realization leads into the high conflict and peak of the play and brings the play to the OBLIGATORY SCENE or the CLIMAX in more modern terms.

The CLIMAX is usually the most active scene and brings the characters to the culmination of the final confrontation, physical and/or emotional peak, with the uncertainty of who will win. This pivotal scene is the point of no return and builds to the highpoint of the CLIMAX between the protagonist and the antagonist and directly to the end of the story.

The scene of the final unraveling of the story in which the plot is resolved to a new reality, leads to the conclusion of the tale. The END shows the way life will be now, and everyone lives happily, sadly or tragically ever after. This END is best when it is very brief and gets quickly to the point, especially in children's theater. For adult audiences the END may be a bit more specific and a little broader in detail, but still should not go on and on too long as in an extended *Denouement*.

Nonlinear Stories

The events of the more modern nonlinear plays occur outside of a specific time line and often without a specific storyline. These plays are often presented with various events occuring and scenes may or may not relate to each other obviously as they are played. Events jump from idea to idea, and end without a connective scene to bring the play to an explanatory or a decisive ending. The play may be left with an open conclusion for the audience to determine for itself.

This unraveled format could be appropriate and delightful to audiences of all ages. However, to be successful and work as a piece of theater, it must still be one, complete, perhaps unraveled, but whole world within itself. It may not be the world of reality, but all the parts must belong and relate to the events within the play as a whole.

A single event or series of events within a given situation outside of a specific tale or several tales blended, in or out of sequence. A play might begin with the climax and vary its way from past to present not necessarily following a specific time plan. Any play could jump from one scene to another place, and other events important to the tale, but offered out of time sequence, still within the story of the play. This broken sequence of time and place may be rich and thrilling to third grade and up, and certainly for adult audiences.

Some nonlinear plays will mix two or three unrelated stories or events with scenes entangled and relating one to another with the characters in one scene involved in actions in a totally unrelated story, scene or event. The ending must, in some way, bring all the events of the play or major characters to a unified conclusion.

Film uses techniques that live stage actors cannot easily achieve, such as "jump shots" where there is a situation happening in one place or scene, then jump to a different location or time but featuring one or more actors from the previous scene.

Puppet theater may also move quickly from one scene, or one set of characters to another. Cinderella may appear in her ball gown dancing with the Prince and the clock begins to chime at midnight. At the same moment she may appear on stage with her Godmother, as a memory, reminding her to leave the ball by midnight. This image could be larger or smaller than the puppet, flat pictorial or sculptured as are the regular puppets. The gowned Cinderella must then react to the memory, note the time on the clock and run off, losing her slipper as she goes, thus setting the play for the next actions. This scene may be accomplished with only one line of dialogue from the Fairy Godmother.

A memory or dream sequence might be shown in a background image in shadows. An almost instant change of scenery, an instant change of costume, an instant flip-flop from one scene to another and back again in moments. Anything is possible in puppetry, as are back flashes or forward leaps in time or tale. These techniques are very important in contemporary puppet theater.

In puppet theater there are many ways to change scenery with little more than a flip of the hand, the pull of a string, the twist of a knob or a projected photographic setting. A puppet may pop up or down onto the stage *if* that is appropriate for the story telling, characters and situations. Certainly Punch and Judy may pop up and down and Judy may be killed, rise from being dead and tease Punch into believing she is a ghost. A dream sequence may appear on stage over a sleeping puppet figure in many ways as may happen in cartoons, film and television.

Exclamation points, question marks or light bulb "ideas" may pop up over a figure's head, and while these specific given images are dated and trite, the visual *idea* is not. Often the dated and trite images may be highly entertaining, but overuse will quickly become a bore.

A memory or dream sequence might be shown in a background image in shadows. An almost instant change of scenery, an instant change of costume, an instant flip-flop from one scene to another and back again in moments. Anything is possible in puppetry, as are back flashes or forward leaps in time or tale. These techniques are very important in contemporary puppet theater. Plays for puppet theater must be appropriate to the audience, the puppet style, but they must also be good theater.

Plays for puppet theater must be appropriate to the audience and the puppet style The difference is in the functioning, style and use of the artificial puppet as opposed to the living human actors. The actors work to understand and re-create the characters they are playing. The puppets are symbolic representations or illustrations of the characters the puppeteer is communicating and sharing with the audience.

Punch and Judy

15 Building Blocks for Plays

The basic elements in the creation of a play are: Premise, Plot, Vision (Idea), Character, Dialogue, Spectacle, Climax and a brief Conclusion, and the Curtain Call. These nine elements are the essentials of any form of story theater including puppetry. While these elements must be dealt with in any theatrical scripting, they may be stressed at variable levels of importance. Together they form the whole of a play, and each element must be developed artfully in order for the show to communicate with the audience.

Premise, simply stated, is the playwright's voice, the idea, the inspiration. This voice may be a philosophy, a theory, an attitude about various aspects of life, theater or puppetry. The premise is not related to the plot line but may still affect it and all other aspects of the play. An experienced writer does not usually need to think about premise, as it will automatically come into being through creative and thoughtful writing.

While the premise is reflected within the play, it must not control or force it, but rather inspire it and give it form. For example, Mary Churchill of the Cranberry Puppets was very concerned about the treatment and mistreatment of women in many stories. Her feminist perceptions were important, but she did not want to belabor the tales with her philosophy. Yet she often changed the stories to show strong female characters without overtaking the story with her philosophy.

Vision is the unification of the many ideas behind and within the needs of storytelling blended into a single conception or overall view. What will make the play rich and exceptional puppet theater as opposed to human theater? What format will it take? Comedy, tragedy, adventure, knock about comedy or other form or a blending of ideas within the play? How are the visual aspects of design, coloring and the elements of the play intended to affect the story? Will it be modern, historic, antique, stylized, fantastic, unreal, almost abstract? The design must be consistent within itself but variable in mood changing scenes.

When is the play happening in time? Where in space? How in organization? How will the scenery, costumes, coloration, properties and overall design affect the audience within this specific play? The visual design of the whole must be in harmony with everything else in the play, the whole of the idea is usually one image shared with the audience.

Will the audience be aware of the performers creating the tale? Is the actor visible with the puppet being manipulated? If so, will he or she also appear as a costumed character in the play? What role does the puppeteer take?

Creative imagination is a strong key to everything within the whole of the play, because the play is only one thing ... Itself.

Plot is the story line of the play. Plot shapes the storyline and communicates what happens to whom and by whom and why, how and what are the affects of these happenings on the characters and especially on the story being revealed. It is all the events relating to the one story, the tale that makes for good enriching theater.

In a brief puppet play there is no time or space for subplots, scenes or activities outside of the plot or the play's primary idea. Most plays for child audiences stress plot over characterization. Both must be there, of course, but plot and its events are usually far stronger. The reverse is often true for adult audiences who are more likely to connect with the characterization more than the plot line although they both must work as one.

Characterization is the deep and conscious creation of the various human, animal, mineral, vegetable or imagined creatures involved and represented within the play. It is the art of developing rich, believable and acceptable personalities within the story. For younger children the characters are usually simplified and less complex. They must be easily recognized and far less complex than in plays for teens or adults, who prefer an understanding and a presentation of the various characters' inner personalities, deeper almost instinctive emotions, mental or personal needs. In most plays, especially in plays for child or family audiences, there *must* be at least one character whom the audience will appreciate, love and care about. It may be a child, adult, an animal, or invented creature which is involved in the successful or happy ending to the play.

Dialogue may or may not be used dependent on the author's needs or wants. When dialogue is used, it must be kept simple, expressive of each individuals' emotional, mental and personal needs and the demands of the other aspects within the play. Dialogue is the verbal and emotional communication between the characters to express the needs of the characters and the tale. If dialogue is not used, the puppet gestures must be enriched by emotional actions and reactions within the script in order for the actions and nonverbal motivations to express the characters and their reasons for their activation.

In either case, movement is the major element. Movement is mightier than words! There is nothing more boring than two characters having long conversations about what is happening off stage, unseen by the audience. In cases where this is the only conceivable way to present the scene, the movement and dialogue must be done with high choreographic visual and emotional energy and vital communication and sharing.

Spectacle occurs during the various high points within the play. It is the discovery of what is causing change(s) within their life styles or situations. These may be physical, mental, emotional, verbal or highly imaginative or any combination or all of these qualities at once. This spectacular activity is usually the highest tension point of action and the peak of the story. The climax is the most powerful event. Every play must have some turning point. In the best productions there is a balance between different types of emotional scenes (sorrowful, worried, hopeless) and high scenes (eventful, angry, happy) or other varieties of activity appropriate to the events within the tale.

The **End** is the final brief expression or suggestion of the world resulting from the events in the play. How will the main characters respond to the new world? Will there be an emptiness in their lives or will they live happily ever after? Will the new way of life be, a wonderful change, a different unknown but adventurous future or a life of toil and mystery? This END is best when kept very brief and to the point.

The **Curtain Call** is part of any play. It is a form of "Thank You" between the performers and the audience. Whether casual, informal or formal, it should usually match the artistry and intent of the rest of the performance. perhaps, demonstrate some of the puppets. Opinions vary about demonstrating some of the puppets , but in my experience, it is improper to show too many puppet secrets after the performance. Like a magician, there are techniques the puppeteer ought not to reveal. One wants to leave the audience at a peak of energy from the drama. Revealing too much of how and why may easily spoil the power of the play and weaken the *Art* of puppetry to playtime. Never allow children of an audience to touch or play with the puppets, props or any of the equipment. The puppets and the skills to manipulate them are simply too valuable.

16   Routines for Character Development

The Nobody should be on the performer's writing hand for the first pieces, then redo the pieces with the puppet on the non-writing hand. A good performer needs as much skill and vitality performing with either or both hands at once.

Changes may be made in the routine if desired or needed for variation or improvement with the non-writing hand, or just to do it in a different way because different is good for learning, too. A performer may render the pieces as written or change them to a character behaving impromptu.

Never (Repeat: *NEVER)* read from a written script when performing. It is impossible to read, act, manipulate a puppet and communicate with an audience at the same time. If some part of the practice piece is left out, let it go, or improvise something to fill in the gap. Become the mind behind what is happening with the puppet on your hand, not, necessarily, what it says in the script.

Most of these studies say: *he*. The puppet may be he, she, or anyone or anything. Every character has gender, age, personality and in classic theater for adults, the characters have life histories from birth to the end of the play. Some of the characters could be animals or out of this world others, or what does the imagination crave? Create!

Scenes

Note: The first scene is done three times to suggest possible character variations. There are thousands of possibilities to every skit ... I mean "dramatic theater pieces."

> ENTER PUPPET. He waves to the audience, to the left, the right and stage center. He claps his hands and blows a kiss or two to the audience, waves and EXITS.

Who is the person coming on stage? It could be anyone, but whoever the puppeteer decides, that character must be a true and consistent character. Every scene has its own specific characters.

Idea Variations:

1. A Super Rock Star might bound onto the stage boldly waving and blowing kisses to the cheering teen audience. He might run to the center, arms wide and welcoming, clapping to his fans, He blows kisses as he exits bounding exuberantly off stage like a true super star.

2. An Opera Diva would enter with a great deal more elegance. She might enter grandly, slowly walk to center stage, where she might curtsy deeply to the cheering audience and throw kisses, then elegantly rise and throw more kisses out to the audience. With one last kiss and wave, she exits behind the curtain with rich and dignified finesse.

3. A Young Boy who had never been on stage or in front of an audience, would be nervous and scared and might wave shakily. He might blow an awkward kiss in embarrassment or just awkwardly. Perhaps he blows a kiss to his family or someone he recognizes. He has forgotten

what he was supposed to say, fumbles not knowing what to do and runs off stage.

For all the skits, begin with the emotional *"Who"* is entering the stage. Make all the scenes responsive for a specific character. It is not only *what* is happening, it is also *who* is causing the what, how and why. The puppeteer must understand the *why* and *how* they do their moves will create many variable possibilities.

Give some clues to the audience about *who* the puppet character is.

It is important (and fun) to be specific and detailed, the performer may improvise even in the first tries. Every character is a specific, a someone, doing something for intentional or accidental reasons. When acting out and plotting these very simple pieces, it is important to plan, plot and finagle to make each playlet as sharp and important as possible. One is not *doing* the skits, one is *recreating* them, continuously.

On with More Scenes

1. The Puppet enters, He is looking for something. He looks here and there. He is upset that he cannot find the item. He searches repeatedly, but then he finds it. He is very happy. He picks up the item and happily carries it off.

2. Puppet enters and is very sad. He sits down slowly, and thinks sadly and cries. The crying grows into heavy keening. Slowly the crying subsides. He wipes his eyes, gets up and walks off sadly.

3. The Puppet runs on. He stops suddenly and looks left and right, and upstage. He realizes he is going the wrong way. He thinks a moment. He cannot remember which way. He struggles with the memory, He decides which way to go. He turns, points and runs off.

4. The Puppet enters eagerly looking for something. He looks here and there and becomes increasingly upset. He cannot find it. He looks almost hysterically for it. At last he cries and walks off empty handed.

5. Puppet creeps on. He looks about to be sure that no one is following him. He looks from side to side and finds that he is alone. He rubs his hands, laughs wickedly and tiptoes sneakily off to do his deed.

6. Puppet walks on stage. He trips and falls. He tries to get up but there is pain. Struggling, he gets up and starts to cry. He rubs his painful knee and limps off in pain.

7. Puppet jumps down and lands clumsily onstage. He gets up and looks around for a friend. He searches, and looks until He sees the friend far away. He waves to the friend and dashes to join him, and trips, in his eagerness, catches himself, and runs off.

8. Puppet walks on looking for someone. He sits down and waits. He taps the stage impatiently and looks around for the someone. His impatience grows stronger and stronger. He waits some more and then gets up frustrated and angry and storms off angrily.

9. Puppet enters and is very tired. He yawns, stretches. Then he cleans off a spot on the stage and lies down. He goes to sleep and begins to snore. He snores louder and louder. He snores so loudly the he wakes himself up. He gets up, yawns, stretches and walks off.

On the Other Hand

Now put the Nobody on the non-writing hand and do the playlets again. Perform each skit differently. There is no one way to do any of these, be a variable as possible.

Stretch your ideas and use the creative imagination, learning, growing and becoming a performer of greater artistry, richer comedy and more dramatic power.

Groups Working Together: When groups are working together, it is important to offer some form of *Response Sessions*. Viewers should express their likes, positive opinions and suggestions for possible improvement. It is wise to understand these are not critical but learning techniques for helping and correcting in positive ways. It is wise to begin with a compliment or two and then ask questions about a bit that was unclear or make suggestions for some improvements. Repeat or offer new complimentary or positive statements.

Two Nobodies • One Somebody: Now, put a Nobody puppet on each hand and do the sketches below. As a broad guide line, one puppet moves and the second figure pauses. The second figure responds to the first who pauses while the second moves. This helps the audience to see and know what a puppet is doing.

When two puppets are active at the same time, the audience gets confused. They cannot watch two different things at once. If the script says they are walking in together or doing something as one, they move together, but generally, even in a fight, one figure moves, then the second figure responds.

This suggestion also applies when two puppets are talking to each other, one speaks and the other listens and then the second figure answers and the first one listens. Otherwise, the audience will have difficulty knowing what is happening. The hand is quicker than the eye and two hands doing different things at once is not manipulation, it is jiggling, an event that should never happen in good puppet theater.

The puppeteer moves the figures with intelligence, reason and intent. Extremely active movement between two or more characters must be choreographed.

Double Duty Demi-Dramas

Two puppets with one puppeteer and two hands.

1. One Puppet enters looks about and waits. Figure Two enters, looks about and sees figure One. They hurry to each other, shake hands, hug and greet hello. First puppet indicates the second figure should come with him, pointing to something off stage. They walk off together.

2. Two puppets are sleeping. One wakes up and tries to wake the other. The second puppet keeps falling back to sleep repeatedly. The first puppet tries multiple times to wake the first, then he gives up, shrugs in disgust, lies down and goes back to sleep. (Puppets sleeping at the end of a piece, are lifted up a bit with a tuk, and slowly lowered down behind the playboard in a formal exit.) Just whipping them off stage is clumsy, meaningless and very unprofessional. This is a learning process for becoming professional. Nothing is done sloppy or mindless.

3. One puppet enters and is very sad. The second figure comes on and tries to cheer up the sad one. The sad one cries even harder. Then the sad one whispers in the hap

py one's ear. The puppet then also gets sad and the two walk off crying together.

4. Two puppets meet. One starts to cry. The other tries to comfort the crier, finally the crying one starts to giggle and laugh. They laugh together then go off together, laughing happily!

5. One puppet comes on stage slowly. The second creeps up behind him and scares him. The first puppet jumps up in surprise then faints. The second puppet tries several times to awaken the first but cannot. The second drags the fainted figure off stage.

6. One puppet runs on and trips and falls. The second puppet comes on and tries to help the first gets up. They struggle in their efforts and they both fall down off stage and out of sight.

7. One puppet is asleep on stage and snoring peacefully. Another puppet sneaks on and tip toes around, looking for something. The first figure wakes up and tries to catch the first one. The second figure run off with the first one chasing after him.

8. Two puppets meet. They get into a fight, both fall down. They get up and apologize, become friends again, and go off together.

9. Two puppets are walking side by side. One sees something (positive or negative) and tries to make the other look. He won't. The first keeps trying to show the second what it there. Finally they both look then run off together.

10. One puppet is trying to lift something. It is very heavy.
    The figure struggles more. The second figure comes on.
    He tries to help. They cannot lift the item. They struggle,
    but cannot lift it. They try several times to pick it up.
    They cannot. They both go off exhausted.

All of these pieces may be done over differently for experience and learning. Any of these double pantomimes could be done by one puppeteer or two puppeteers. With two performers, the puppet is usually on the outside hand. Some scenes may need them on the same hand. In some cases the reverse will work better. Try it and see. Seek and find. What works best is usually quickly discovered, but always double check. Experimenting teaches a great deal! We can and should learn to teach ourselves and others, to make and break our own rules, to not just make things easy but to make them the best they can be. Try to invent some of your own practice pantomimes and skits. Take it where it goes!

If a piece doesn't work at first, find a way to make it work and do it again.

There is no one way to do anything. Experiment, change, add, delete.

17 Etudes in B#

An *etude* is a short puppet study. *Etude* sounds so much better than skit and a great deal better than variety act. "A nose by any other name may stop and smell the roses!" (Apologies Mr. Shakespeare!) Earlier in the book, we did exercises to develop characters. Here the focus will be on a more full view of the show, including characterization but also the plotting and visionary elements discussed in the previous few chapters.

It is important to begin writing and performing small, simple playlets before creating the masterpiece. The *etudes* may be striking and heart gripping performances of one and a half minutes, or a bit longer as needed in the playing. Hamlet said, *Brevity is the soul of wit*. (Brevity is also very difficult to do well.) The *etude* piece occurs in one scene and in a brief time span and focuses on of one basic idea. Like any play, long or short, it must still have a beginning, a middle and an end, but it is kept simple using, often one or two characters, and sometimes, like a painting, may contain some unexplained secret. These brief theatrical sketches are fine puppet theater in its simplest form.

These etudes might be a revelation of a special character, a touching moment of drama, a hilarious comic situation. A character doing its own thing with a problem needing to be solved.

Whatever the mood, these brief etudes must avoid being corny or empty bits of drivel. They might be made to enrich, entertain and capture the audience before the play begins. In any of these short skits it is not only what the skit is about, it is how well it is done. A bad dog act is a bore, a good dog act can be amazingly humorous and highly entertaining.

One must be certain the puppet seems to feel the emotions of the skit, and not just the words and physical actions.

Puppeteers often say the idea is the only thing, that good ideas make good puppetry. I wholly disagree. The good idea is a great beginning, not the finished work. Begin with a good idea and turn it into a fine piece of delightful or tragic puppet theater with thought, belief, voice, movement and mood and end with the audiences cheering at curtain call.

In a very short playlet the elements of theater must still be there, simplified and selective, but there. Simplicity, too, is usually more important in these short plays than complexity. Another quote from the wise vital thinker, Albert Einstein; "Everyone should do everything as simply as possible, but no simpler than that."

As one begins crafting an etude, questioning is a vital part of discovery. Begin with one or two characters, a prop and some sort of relationship must happen between the object and the characters. The scripts may be done with or without dialogue. They may be comical, tragical, musical, rebellious, or whatever and wherever the imagination may wander.

Perhaps the character is a tramp or hobo. There is a tree with one bright red apple in the tree. The tramp wants, needs, longs for that apple! How does he go about trying to get the apple? How many attempts does he try. What happens when he tries? Does he jump up a few times? Does he fall? How else might he try? A ladder? A box to stand on? A stick to knock the ball from the tree? Does he get the apple or not? Either way, how does he exit, happily or sadly? In one version the tramp, after many unsuccessful attempts to reach the apple, and several painful falls, leaves, hurt, hungry and sad, and after the tramp is gone, the apple slowly descends to the ground, and the tree laughs heartily.

One basic format for developing an etude is: the character enters, finds an object. The object objects. There is a brief imbalance between them. There must be some conflict between the *Character* and the *Object*. The character can win and the object can lose, the character can lose and the object win, both may win or both may lose, depending on the script, the choreography and the intent of what is communicated with the audience.

Etudes may be musical. A lovely singer enters, pats her lovely hairdo and walks in to center stage, her gown swishing and swirling as she walks. She begins to sing. She can sing magnificently (briefly), comedically, egotistically, crazily, off key, insanely over dramatically, showing off to the audience or whatever the performer wants to share with the audience. If the performing puppeteer has singing skills, all the better! Remember this is not a singing act but an etude, a dramatic bit or a comical bit with singing as its *starting* point and part of the content of the study. Where it goes and how it ends is up to the creator.

The *etudes* or studies may be done with or without dialogue. They may not be done without theatricality! The important thing is to really work them out with full feelings and emotions generated by the simple small showpiece. Also these very short pieces usually have one basic idea that needs to be communicated, dealt with, interrupted, and ended with problems solved, left unresolved or leading into other new problems. All art is a lie that tells the truth. What is the truth of the act? Wherein lies the lie?

In the playing of an etude one learns to act, edit, cut and adjust in a brief skit before tackling a major theater production. Many fine playwrights have learned their craft by writing short one act plays before moving on to longer plays as they learned. Anton Chekov did many short comic bits and one act plays before he attempted to write a full length play.

If one needs a place to start, there are many Shakespearian scenes which can stand alone and be done by puppets. Lady Macbeth's *Sleep Walking Scene* is a frequent flyer. The important thing is to read the entire play (or a very well done synopsis) to find the reasons, actions and causes within the scene. Understanding the characters and their reasons for their actions will make the scenes true to life even if edited and manipulated in nonrealistic ways with nonrealistic puppets. The choices and possibilities are unlimited.

There are many books of short scenes for actors to use as audition pieces. These scenes often work for puppets but may need some trial and adaptation.

No matter your source material, artful adaptation is key. Martin Stevens, the master-puppeteer, well known in the nineteen thirties and forties for his full length productions of Shakespearean plays with marionettes, was teaching a class on playwriting for puppet theater. He told his class. "If one is writing a script from a book or even from human theater, it is absolutely necessary to rewrite and change the story and movement in ways that are especially suitable to puppet theater." A woman in the class raised her hand and asked, "My plays are all taken from the Bible. Is it permissible to rewrite the Bible?"

Mr. Steven's brilliant reply was, "Of course you can rewrite the Bible. Why, I even rewrite Shakespeare!" Mr. Stevens denied ever saying such a thing, but he has been given full credit for it by other students who took the class. How I wish I had said that line!

Current news events, political satire, human interest, adventures or social situations that are happening all the time around us. The key words are dramatic, comic, romantic, adventurous, tragic, hilarious, imaginative, original, creative, sexual, goofy, religious, pastoral, political, terrifying, fun or magnificent and a million other creative formats.

Never go for the obvious, the inane, the silly or the all too often done. Avoid the great *"Ho hum!"* Go for vibrant puppet theater for children or for adults. Very short pieces will give a new puppeteer the experience and information needed before writing a full play.

Making Etudes into a Full Play

Once you've developed a complete etude, these studies may be strung together as a series to make a full length performance, usually with a central theme.

Making a series of scenes in a park setting might be very interesting. Who gathers in the park? Where does the conflict occur? Is it a sad piece or a very happy situation? What happens in a park that could make an interesting and moving theater sketch? Gossip? Children playing well or badly? Elderly people gabbing about whatever?

Some sponsors of puppetry want a performance to last about one hour, others may want forty-five minutes, and others a brief thirty minutes. For a longer piece it may be a short play of thirty minutes with the shorter small plays or etudes filling in the desired time. It is far better to put the variety pieces at the beginning of the performance as an introduction to the play. A few simple comic or entertaining interludes may hold the attention and the audience is then ready for the longer story.

Once the main story is over the audience is ready to applaud and leave, and the variety numbers tacked at the end often go unappreciated.

Many performers create an entire show with these brief puppet theater etudes. Some put the brief scenes imaginatively within the scope of the play or story itself. Dick Myers always put *"Some entertainment"* pieces within his storied plays. They were always fun and very humorous bits of theatricality. This type of playing one way before the play and another way during the play has happened repeatedly since the very beginning of theater.

Again, it is strongly repeated: A grand idea is a great beginning but good theater is the final goal. The important things are, these acts must be well performed, well conceived, and theatrically meaningful.

18 Write It Down

Logos, Letterheads & Information

All professional companies should have an attractive and memorable logo image. It may be a photo of a puppet, a symbolic or pictorial logo image, a pen and ink sketch, a special type face of the name or whatever identification image the company uses. The image may be formal or informal, but must look well-planned, intentional and professional. Neatness is an essential, artistry is a luxury.

Good photographs of the puppets always attract attention. Do not do photos with a puppet on each hand on either side of your head. Make the photo professional, attractive and interesting, and avoid being boring or typical.

Every company needs a good, well designed letterhead. Generally the letterhead information takes up no more than two-and-a-half to three inches at most, leaving plenty of room for written information, contracts, proposals and any other needed or shared information.

Make sure all the other documents for your business – request forms, contracts, business cards – have deep attention to professionalism and artistry, just like your performance.

Brochures and Fliers

Brochures must be interesting enough to make a potential customer pick it up to read. An eye catching photo, interesting art work, beautiful drawing or whatever. Use compelling colors or other decoration. Whatever the look, it should be in good contemporary design and very legible.

Think professional in any flyer, advertisement, or brochure. Do not go cute or childlike. An adult will be hiring and paying for the program for children. The brochure must appeal to the adults involved.

The flyer must contain the name of the puppet company, some information and photographs of the various plays and the name of the person(s) in charge, the address, telephone and/or cell phone, and if desired, an Email or other on-line address. You can also include reviews of your work.

Never quote prices on any printed brochure or advertisement piece because the prices will certainly change. The times change, the money available to possible clients varies, and often the needs of the puppet company will change over time. A potential client may have an old flier, if that outdated flyer shows an old price range, many will want the old price rather than the new and (hopefully) higher price. Most clients want the cheapest prices possible.

Copies of every brochure, flyer, or anything published, every advertisement and all contract forms should have the printing date (in small type) for one's own future information. Many professionals will come across old brochures or advertising folders and cannot remember when or where they were published. A tiny date somewhere is a boon, even a copywrite date.

Business Cards

Business cards are quite useful and valuable. Have business cards printed with the company logo, the name, address, phone numbers, email and website information. Anything concerning puppet theater must look and contain professional information.

It is wise not to have to fumble in your pocket or purse to find the cards. Have them in their own case and carry them in a chest pocket or any place one may take them out easily and confidently.

Many puppet companies hand cards to anyone willing to take them. The advantage of a well designed business card is it will sometimes go to the right people for the right reasons. The disadvantages are it may also get into the wrong hands. You need to be able to deal with unlikely customers in a professional and engaging manner.

Date everything!

Every letter, every contract and all publicity data needs a current date on the forms. It is also wise to put a publishing date on brochures, post cards, printed performance programs, and all printed documents to recall when they were published. One can forget when brochures, or other items were published and finding even a very small date will clue one in, for possible future or current use or for disposal.

Again, never publish prices in brochures or pamphlets about the company. Costs for performances and travel often change and pre-published prices can easily become problematic. Save everything: reviews of your shows, (both raves and pans), printed or written comments from clients or even friends. Positive statements or any favorable comments from employers are saved on computer, cell phones or whatever mechanism is currently available.

Information Forms

Most professional puppet companies have special forms to fill in when booking a show on the telephone or from a website. This form, printed on white paper, requests the following information and includes spaces to complete the hand-written or word processed answers. (Does anyone use typewriters any more?)

- Performance Date(s),
- Event,
- Hiring organization,
- Contact name,
- Contact address,
- Space for at least two pertinent Telephone Number(s) and Cell Phone numbers,
- Email address,
- Fax Numbers (Are they still in use?),
- Performance information such as, audience ages, audience size, show title, length of performance, arrival time, start time, price, contract phone number, performance location, directions and, especially, date of most recent phone call. It is also wise to ask how the potential client heard about your company and have a computer file or a printed form for the information.

Contracts

It is important to have a contract form printed on the business letterhead. It should include the names and contact information of both the puppet company and the hiring organization.

Performance information includes: the dates, times and address(es) of the performance(s), and the name(s) of the person(s) dealing with the performance(s). Two copies should be prepared and signed by both parties - the client keeps one and returns the other to the performing company.

The contract must also contain a line saying something approximating: "The (puppet company name), in an emergency, has the right to change the title and/or content of the performance without previous notice."

It is very important for the performer to have that signed contract with them at the performance in case of problems or disagreements with the clients. The contract is basic and legal in the case of small claims court law suits by the performing company or the hiring company for proof of any breach of contract.

Many puppet companies will have a line that reads similar to: "Cancelation by the client within (X number of business days) of the performance date, the total fee is due to the performing company." Some performing companies do not have that clause and others may ask for a percentage rather than the full fee. These choices are flexible, but clients can and often do change a contract on whim, or whatever, or because someone else offers a lower price, a title the client likes better, or whatever may occur. A signed and dated contract is legally binding. With a signed contract, in most cases, one may insist on full payment or sue in a small claims court.

All signed contracts are valid and must be accommodated.

Never cancel a booking because you get a better offer for that date. A performance date is sacred once the contract is signed by both parties, no matter what. The show must go on.

Be highly professional about setting dates, contracts and arriving at venues on time. It is the professional way to go. All puppet companies, whether a solo performer or a company with a larger number of performers, must have full coverage in case the puppet company has turned down other bookings because they have already accepted the gig.

In this case it is unlikely the puppeteers can regain those losses, unless the contract has legally binding signatures by performer and hiring agent in any cases of dispute. If possible, have a professional business lawyer check your document for legal accuracies. Be careful, however, not to get the contract so full of legalese that the clients will not read it. A good contract is expressive in its intent but simple, easy to read and understand.

Do not perform for any customer without a signed and dated contract in hand.

Attachments to the Contract

Many puppeteers have an attachment sheet of the space required for stage and equipment.

Include other performance needs, such as height of the ceiling, size of the stage space needed, and any other special needs of the puppet company such as nearby 120 volt, 20 amp outlets. Also include special needs for your company such as: the puppet stage must be against a wall or backdrop rather than in front of a window or a frequently trafficked entryway.

A sketch of the stage with measurements is also helpful and useful as part of the contract.

Customers often have no idea of good or appropriate performing space needs. It is also helpful to gain certain information like which door you go to for entrance and installing your equipment, where you should park, or any other needs when you arrive at the appointed place and time.

This does not have to be in writing but is helpful information: Directions to the locale from the clients are often confusing and frequently with some important information left out.

It is also wise to find the locale on a map or an electronic travel guide in the vehicle.

Another attachment to the contract may include study guides for teachers at school performances. These study guides may aid some teachers in talking about the show afterwards and information useful in their class rooms.

When one becomes rich and famous most of these details are taken care of by an agent, and the professional performer has only to deal with that representative. Oh joy!

Study Guides

Good study guides are a major need for performers who choose to perform for schools.

Study guides might include such personal things as complimentary quotes from previous clients, personal information about the performer(s). Study guides are to help teachers use your performance for special activities in the classes room. Include such things as listing some books about puppet theater, or give information for the children to make voices for different characters, etc.

If telling a story from a specific country, give study information about the country. Be accurate with facts. Or find studies about folk and fairy tales or other information which offers the teachers interesting ideas for reading or writing about fairy tales. Or explore whatever the puppet performance incvludes that could be used for educational purposes. Make the study guide both educational and, of course, fun at the same time.

These study guides must be interesting and very well done to inspire the teachers to use them and to keep your work and quality in mind.

The Red Ball,
an anti-war protest piece for adult audiences.

19 Be a Pro

A strong professional attitude is extremely important. It shows respect for the art, and it completes the artistry of the performance. One must act and look professional to potential clients, to the audience, and to all concerned. It is wise to begin to learn the intent of professional attitudes, behavioral skills and habits, even as you begin to learn to perform.

Establishing a Puppet Company

The name of the puppet company is very important. The name must be compatible with the quality of the work the company is most interested in doing.

Avoid nonsense names or any name suggesting nonsense or foolishness. One may use words suggesting comedy, or fine theater, or whatever, but it should be professional in sound and quality. Make certain the name is as professional as you are as a performer.

Professional Behavior

To be a professional, you must behave professionally. This does not mean you should arrive at a gig dressed in fancy dinner jackets, but at least look clean and neat and not poverty stricken (even if you truly are). Many puppeteers wear black slacks and a Tee shirt or sweater with their puppet company logo. Simple, neat and clean is a look for the self and all professional equipment.

In addition, meeting deadlines, keeping personal relationships out of the rehearsal and performance space, and avoiding drugs and alcohol during performances and rehearsals are all vital ways to be a professional and ensure the artistic integrity of your work.

Additionally, be confident in yourself as an artist. Do not allow a potential client to demand anything that you know will not work or is amateurish. No matter the venue for a performance, the very first and perhaps the most important thing is to be polite, warm and friendly to the crew, while still being certain all of one's professional needs as a performing puppeteer will be properly fulfilled. If there are problems with technical aspects, it is important to insist they meet your standards. Explain and request your professional needs in a polite but strong and knowing way. Do not ask for the impossible nor agree to accomplish the impossible. Always research the venue in advance and examine all the information they give you about the performing space, even where to park. Don't let preventable issues trip you up on the day of the performance.

Caring for Puppets

Professionalism begins in rehearsals. Once the puppeteer's hand goes into the puppet, the fingers, wrist, and arm become the skeleton and muscles of the puppet character. In a sense it is no longer your own arm or hand. You must learn to respect yours own artistic and theatrical equipment. If a person enters during a rehearsal, finish the scene before recognizing the friend. The puppeteer should never wave to the newcomer with a glove puppet on the hand. Make it a habit to think of the hand inside the puppet as "belonging" to the figure. Remove the puppet and wave to the friend with the hand uncovered.

During a performance, when waiting back stage for a scene to begin with the puppets on the hands, one might turn them in and hold them lightly against the chest. One should never "abuse" the puppets by having them dangle upside-down at the ends of the arms, especially if the puppets have flowing costumes of skirts or capes. The performer must be certain the puppet will not enter the stage with its costume draped over its head, and shaking the costume down before an entrance is not a professional act. The professional needs to make a separation between one's personal physical and emotional being and the puppet object's importance to the play, the art form, the audience and the art form of puppetry.

Pack the figures carefully so the painted features do not get scraped or scarred, costumes do not get wrinkled, and other details do not get in disarray. It takes a little more time to pack the equipment carefully, but it is very well worth the effort. It is best to use cloth bags to cover the puppets rather than plastic. A performer is apt to perspire into the puppets during the performance and when packed in plastic the puppets may become moldy and smelly. This is less likely if the puppets are packed in simple cotton fabric bags which be laundered if needed. Most puppet figures cannot be washed or cleaned. Take care of them. The puppets and all other equipment are the artists' method and equipment. They must be kept and carefully tended for performance use and for occasional display.

Professional puppets should never be used for informal or nonperformance fooling around. Never let a child play with or even handle the professional equipment ... EVER! Never let anyone handle the equipment unless they have been trained to do it carefully and professionally. Puppets are performing instruments, like violins, drums or trombones. They are basics of the art form and a major part of the performer's career.

In a professional class of drawing and painting, the professor once remarked, "Never throw away a sketch, even if you do not like it!

Store it, keep it in good condition, save it in a portfolio. Should one ever become famous, scribbles, doodles and notebooks will be of monetary value." The same is true of puppetry. Do not dispose of unused puppets, props, scenery or working sketches of puppets and keep files of the information on each.

Touring • Toting • Traveling

When traveling long distances and stopping in hotels, motels or bed and breakfast establishments, always take the puppets, the sound system, and the lighting equipment into the room with you.

The stage and any large equipment can stay in the car, van or trailer. The puppets cannot be replaced and good sound and lighting systems are expensive. Today many puppeteer's sound system is often a lap top computer, expensive to replace and the contents may not be recoverable. It is always better to be safe than sorry.

Always carry business cards and brochures with you when touring. One never knows who will see the show and want to book the company.

In many performances the puppeteers are dressed in costumes appropriate to a character within the production. Costumes within the play must always be well designed and made professionally and fit properly. They must also be designed to slip on over regular street clothes. In most performance locations, finding a place for costume changing is not in the realm of possibilities. Back stage is the dressing room, and often one cannot strip down to change costumes backstage.

Arriving at the Performance

It is important to know in advance where to park the vehicle with the equipment in it, which door to load in the equipment, and to which person one must announce the performers' arrival. All the above information should be known before the date of the performance. It is also extremely important to be on time arriving for the performance. Many customers will forgive a late arrival, but no one will forgive a no-show or a very late arrival.

"If a play is once begun, never stop it till it's done. Be the audience large or small, do the performance well, or not at all."

The Show Must Go On!

There are, rarely, some who attend a puppet play who will become an intentional heckler attempting to disrupt the show. It is wise to ignore the heckler. The audience will usually shush the heckler because the others are enjoying the show. Often an usher, teacher, presenter of the show can handle the hecklers. If the heckling continues and no one handles the situation, remember most hecklers are looking for attention. If ignored by performers and the rest of the audience, the pests will usually stop.

Only twice in my thousands of performances have I had to stop the show to silence the heckler before going on with the play. Never refuse to continue the performance. That familiar and professional line and a very old but good habit is: The show must go on!

Fire drills in public schools are the disruptive exceptions If there is a fire drill, the puppeteer must go out with the audience in a professional way, and wait with the teachers and children until the end of the drill. Often the fire drill takes enough time so the puppet play is never finished. One must simply dismantle the equipment and pack up the car. Collect the check even if the play was unfinished. The performer came and was ready and willing to perform but was prevented by the fire department. The check must be in hand before one leaves the place of performance.

Curtain Calls

This has been covered earlier, but is very important to stress. After the performance, one must have a planned and well rehearsed curtain call. Professional theater companies, operas, orchestral concerts, ballet companies, and stand up comedy performances all have curtain calls. They are very important both to the performers and the audiences. Remember too, that the curtain call is form of "thank you" between the performers and the audience.

Sometimes one may show or demonstrate the puppets on the stage as part of the curtain call, but never have the audiences up close enough to touch them, and like a good magician, do not share all the tricks of the trade with the audience. The puppets are professional instruments for performance and must be treated as such. A violinist or pianist does not have the instrument take a curtain call, nor do they have audience members come up and play on or with their professional instruments

There is a big difference between a professional performer taking a curtain call after a performance and a workshop for the children. One may share in a workshop for puppeteers, but never for paying audiences. The audience pays to see a good performance, and the curtain call is thanking the audience for their attention and the audience's applause is thanking the performer for a fine piece of theater.

Packing Up, Loading Out

The performance has ended, the curtain calls are over, and the audience is filing out of the auditorium. The theatre crew is anxious to leave. But the puppeteer's work is not finished, There is still the dismantling the puppet stage, packing the puppets and equipment, and loading out. An efficient and practiced routine will make the task faster, ensure everything is safely stored, and confirm to the stage crew the puppeteer is a true professional.

If the dismantling and packing can become a routine chore with each step following in logical order, the puppeteer's mind will be free to reflect on the performance.

Did each scene work at intended? Did the audience respond correctly? Were there moments when their attention began to drift? How might the show be improved before the next performance?

A truly professional puppeteer is always striving to become better.

The End

Androcles and the Lion

Postlude

There is a great deal of information in this book that is very difficult to accomplish.

Certainly, the art of puppetry is not a foolish or silly activity. It is an art. Working with the many ideas and suggestions, one must be the very best that one is capable of being. Puppetry has been referred to as very fine and luxurious art in many ages past. Let us all work to bring fine puppet theater back into the adult world of theater as well as for various ages of children, teens and families.

In the nineteen twenties, thirties and very early forties, there were many professional puppet companies performing throughout the United States, including Tony Sarg, Bil Baird, Rufus and Margot Rose and many others entertained across the country. Film changed all this when it popularized psychological drama which is beyond the of art of puppet theater, and many marionette and other puppet artists had to change venues to nightclubs, speakeasies and television. Burr Tilstrom of Kukla, Fran and Ollie, presented shows on television for twenty-five years. Live puppet theater was very much reduced in popularity.

There is, of course, room for both fun and fine arts, but at the time of this writing, fine art is fading rapidly in popularity in many parts of the United States. Support for puppetry as art is difficult to find, difficult to explain to non-puppeteers who tend to think of puppet theater as "cute" and "kiddy" entertainment rather than as an engaging art form.

It is important for all artists to discuss, think about, agree with delight, and disagree on thoughtful points of art works and artistry. These many thoughts are mostly my views and also the views of many puppeteers I know and communicate with about puppetry. Some of these ideas are presented in this book. My hopes, dreams and desires are to encourage puppet theater to be the very best that it has been in times gone by and may become again in the future.

I am proud of my work as a performing puppet artist. Though I am no longer performing professionally, I am still a strong believer in the possibilities and artistry of puppetry. Not everyone will agree with my statements or suggestions. Agreements, disagreements, ideas and suggestions and critical evaluations and even disapproving and arguing various aspects of the art, are vitally important between artists and performers.

Thank you and good artistry and success to all who care, give and share. Please write and tell me what you think at the website listed above. I care very much about puppetry as a fine theater art and I hope many others also want to see puppetry blossom again into a vital form of theater art. For all of those who agree and those who disagree, thank you for sharing your ideas. I, too, may change my mind or feelings over time about many details and small things. The large ones are the art and process of professional performance, but times and viewpoints are always changing, and I must also keep up with modern day changes in this fantastic art of puppet theater.

                                        Paul Vincent Davis
                                        Artist in Residence Emeritus
                                        Puppet Showplace Theater,
                                        32 Station Street,
                                        Brookline, Massachusetts 02445-7933

Master artist Paul Vincent Davis is widely recognized as one of America's foremost glove puppeteers. For thirty years he served as Artist in Residence at Puppet Showplace Theater where he and Mary Churchill worked tirelessly to establish a vibrant home for puppetry in New England. Paul created over a dozen full-length puppetry productions and received five prestigious UNIMA-USA Citations of Excellence for his work. Paul was also honored with the President's Award for Lifetime Achievement by the Puppeteers of America. Now retired from performing, Davis remains active as a teacher and mentor in the New England puppetry community.

www.ingramcontent.com/pod-product-compliance
Lightning Source LLC
Chambersburg PA
CBHW060513300426
44112CB00017B/2654